Silent Screams

Rose Eads

Table of Contents

Prologue

Have you ever sat and thought of a story about a young child who endured some form of extreme trauma that you've heard or read about? Or of a child you knew personally? Whether that abuse was in the form of neglect, malnourishment, physical or sexual abuse, or even emotional abuse? Or maybe a child who has an addicted parent that gets high in front of the child, or even worse, has overdosed in front of that child and had to be brought back to life? Or maybe one that has had a loved one shot or killed in front of them?

Do you ever wonder where that child is today? Or if they were able to recover or heal from that trauma, or are they permanently messed up as a result of what they experienced? Were they able to go on and live a normal life, or do they have limitations as a result of what happened? Did they end up incarcerated or in the mental ward, or are their children now suffering from the same trauma, because they are doing the same things to their children that were done to them? Or maybe that child ended their life or maybe took someone else's life while trying to face the demons that haunt them from the trauma? Or did they break the cycle and thrive for better?

Well, I'd like to tell you a story of a young girl I used to know. This is a story of neglect, a story of abuse, physical, sexual, and emotional. A story of sadness and depression. But also, a story of strength, courage, and determination.

Chapter 1
Birth

Rose made her arrival into the world on January 20th, 1974, weighing in at only 5 pounds 4 ounces. She was born at St. Lukes Hospital in Cedar Rapids, Iowa. Born one month premature, she faced a couple of immediate struggles. She was born with an enlarged heart and a hyaline membrane, which meant that her lungs were unable to work on their own. She was a very sick baby who was in danger of losing her life just as quickly as it had just begun. Thankfully, she had a wonderful team of doctors that worked diligently to keep this tiny baby alive. You see, Rose was the first recipient of a breathing device to aid newborns that her pediatrician and another Doctor developed. This breathing device would provide constant airflow to assist her with breathing until her lungs were fully developed and she was able to breathe on her own. She had a lot of ups and downs, and had in fact had to spend the first three months of her life in an incubator in the hospital.

Eventually her lungs grew stronger and were finally able to function without the assistance of the breathing device. And she had gained enough weight to go home and join the rest of her family. She was the final member of a family that consisted of two older brothers, and her parents.

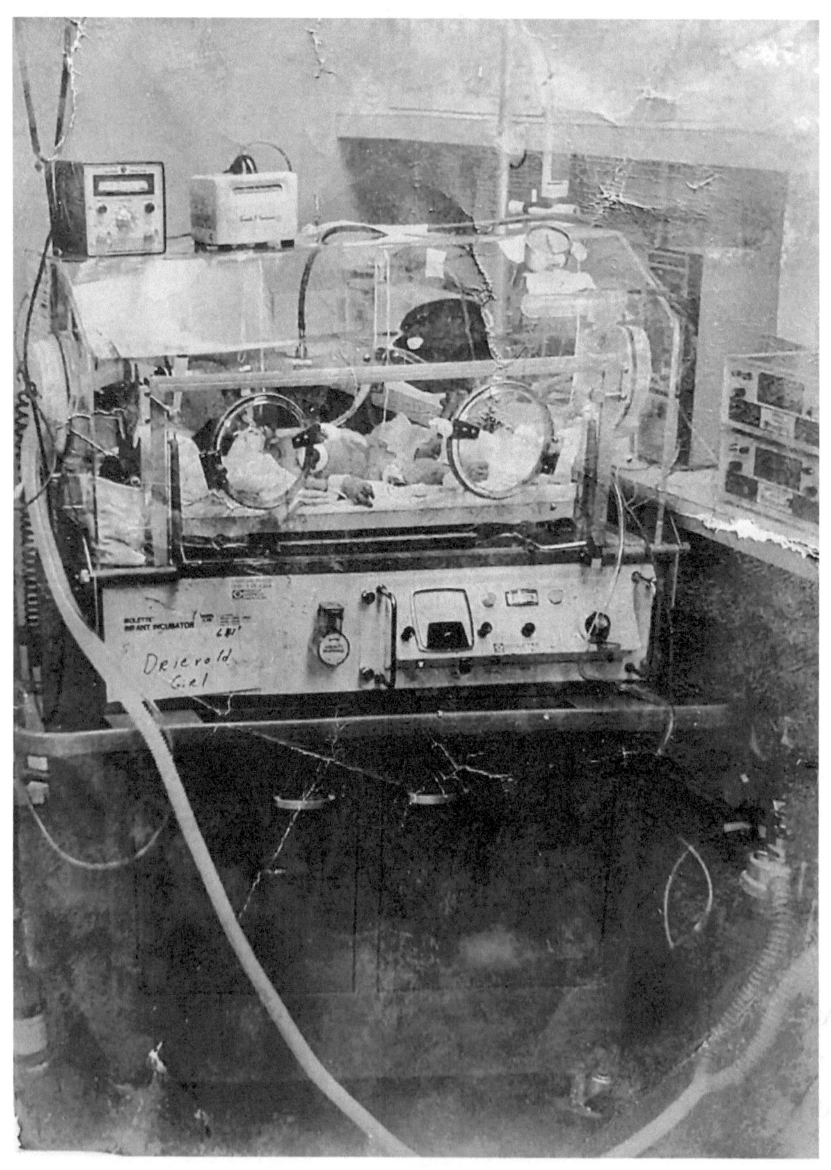
INFANT INCUBATOR
Drierold
Girl

Chapter 2
Age 3

By the age of three, she was a busy, inquisitive, intelligent, thriving, sweet, and sassy toddler who was ready to explore and tackle the world.

You see, we jumped ahead a couple years, because that would be about where her memories began.

She lived with her family in an apartment above a store in Ft. Madison, Iowa. Her bedroom here was a four-season screened porch type room. She didn't remember too much about her family at this stage.

She does, however, remember a cat they had when she lived here. His name was Sam. Sam was a large gold tiger striped tomcat. Rose loved Sam more than anything. Sam was always patient with her and would allow her to do whatever she wanted to him. She would often dress him in baby doll clothes, or put him in her doll cradle. Sometimes, she would even make him sit through a tea party with her baby doll and stuffed animals. Sam was a good sport and would listen to Rose when she would tell him to lay down in the cradle, as a matter of fact, he would stay there until she would take him back out.

He was an extremely intelligent cat. He didn't need a litter box, because he would let himself in and out of the screen door, to use the restroom.

Every night, when it was time for Rose to go to bed, she would call for Sam. "Sam...... here kitty kitty." And he would come jump on her bed and when she laid down, he would snuggle with her, and lay his head across her neck and purr in her ear till they would both go to sleep. Rose does recall one time that her daddy punished Sam for getting on the dining table. And she was really scared that her dad could've killed her cat. Her dad had hit Sam off the table so hard that he hit the wall on the far side of the living room. It must have knocked the wind out of him when he hit the wall, because he just laid on the floor panting and unable to move for a while. Rose was sad that her kitty was hurt. She knew that he didn't mean to get on the table, and he wasn't trying to be naughty. He was just exploring. She made sure to keep him in her room that night, so that he wouldn't cause any more trouble.

At some point, they had acquired a female cat as well. Her name was Sissy, and she was pregnant. Finally, the time would come for her to give birth to her baby kitties.

In most cases, a male cat should not be allowed around a female while she labors, as they may harm or even kill the babies. Not Sam, he sat there comforting her, and even helped to clean the babies off.

He was amazing. Now, Rose doesn't quite recall where the baby kittens had gone, but she did remember that about a month after the babies were born, Sissy lost her life after being struck by a car when she had gotten outside.

She remembered that while living here that there had been a very large rainstorm one day that had caused some flooding in the street as well as in the alley behind the building. She remembers playing in the flooded alley after the rain had stopped that day.

That was about the last of her memories from this house. Except for one memory that came to mind. Rose remembers that her father had started a job at the local steel factory.

Rose's mom would drive her husband and would keep the car in order to drive the kids to appointments and to do errands. One day in particular they loaded in the car. Mom driving, of course, and the three children in the back seat.

Now, just as many young siblings, Rose remembers that she and her brother Jayson would argue and get on each other's nerves. On that day, Rose wasn't happy about sitting in the middle, she wanted to sit by the door so she could look out the window. So, the fight was on. Jayson finally gave in and said, "Fine, you sit by the door then." Rose felt proud that she won the argument, and kinda jumped over her brother's lap as he scooted over.

Now, Rose wasn't quite sure what had just happened or how. Within a matter of moments, she was laying in the street in pain and watched their family car driving away from her. The car quickly turned around and was driving back to her direction.

She was taken to the local hospital and treated for scrapes and bruises, but fortunately no broken bones. She found out, Jayson was tired of arguing with his sister that day. He could see up ahead that his mother was getting ready to turn a corner, so he decided to let her have her way. But, he also decided to do something bad to her to teach her a lesson. You see, what happened that day was that as Rose went to jump over her brother's lap, Jayson pulled the door handle with his left hand and gave her a shove with his right. He was the reason she had fallen out of the car. In fact, he had pushed her out of the car that day.

Jayson was punished for his actions that day, and Rose finally recovered from her injuries.

Chapter 3
Age 4

Rose and her family moved out of the apartment and moved to a house that was about two blocks from the prison. The kids often walked down the two-block hill from their house to the station for their parents. One day, while coming back up the hill from the gas station, it was Rose's turn to carry the eight-pack of glass bottles of their parent's soda. The soda was awkward and heavy to carry, and she had to keep switching which hand she was carrying it in because the cardboard handle was digging into her tiny little fingers.

About halfway back up the hill that day, Rose tripped over a piece of sidewalk that was slightly elevated and the glass bottles slammed against the concrete, and a couple of the bottles broke, which resulted in getting chunks of glass in Rose's hands.

It wasn't long after they moved to this house that Rose remembered having chicken pox. She remembers that her mom would put socks on her hands in an effort to try to get her to stop scratching the bumps all over her body. But it was really hard not to scratch, because the bumps never stopped itching. She also remembered that occasionally, when the boys were at school, her daddy would take her to the store to buy her a special treat.

Which generally consisted of some ice cream or candy. She was told not to tell the boys, but when the boys would come home, she would go running up to them and say, "Ha-ha, I got ice cream today, and you didn't get any." Well let's just say her mom had told her dad not to buy her any more special treats if she was going to brag about it. However, since she was Daddy's girl, he still got her treats until her mom said that if he was gonna buy her anything, he had to buy the boys something, also.

One night, Rose recalled that she was up late helping her mom with laundry while the boys were asleep for school, and her dad was working the third shift at the local steel plant. As Rose and her mom were coming back upstairs, one of the times that night, after switching the laundry, her mom stopped suddenly, and when she did, rose almost fell back down the steps. Something had startled her mother. She tells her daughter, "Shhh," as she catches her daughter's arm, saving her from falling. Now, Rose could hear what had startled her mother. There was somebody pounding on the side door off of the kitchen. As he was pounding, he was yelling, "Open the door, let me in." Well, they weren't expecting any company since it was the middle of the night. She and her mother just sat quietly, hoping that he would go away. But he had made his way to the front of the house. He was now banging on the front door, and the windows in the living room. Her mother told her to go wake her brothers, so she ran upstairs as fast as she could and told her brothers that someone was trying to break in, and that mom wanted them to come downstairs. As they came down the stairs, their mother was holding a butcher knife and told the kids to keep quiet. The guy continued banging for about another 5 minutes. Their mother then watched the silhouette of the man who walked to the road, got into a car, and drove away.

She told Jayson and Rose to run across the street to the neighbor's house and pound on the door until someone answered. Then the lady was asked to please call the police, as well as call her husband to come home from his job. She told them to stay across the street until the police arrived. The two children were terrified. What if that man came back?

Reluctantly, they did as they were told. Their oldest brother said to his mom, "Don't worry, Mom, I'll protect you. Come to find out later, when the officers arrived and knocked on the door, he hid between the back of his mother's legs and the cabinet.

When the officers arrived, they had to pry the butcher knife from their mother's hands. It was a very scary experience for everyone involved.

Thankfully, the man never returned, and Rose's father was now home. The entire family slept in the living room that night.

It wasn't long after this event that Rose remembered a milk-drinking contest with her brother Jayson. The two children were hanging out in the kitchen, and Rose was squirming around as she needed to use the restroom. As she decided she better go use the restroom, Jayson asked, "Hey sissy, do you wanna have a milk drinking contest to see who can drink a glass of milk the fastest?" Rose, being the youngest, always liked an opportunity to show her brothers up. "Sure," she yelled back to him. "After I go pee." Now when Rose would go upstairs to use the restroom, she usually messed around in the bathroom for a while. So Jayson knew he had plenty of time to prepare the glasses of milk.

Rose finally came bouncing down the stairs and joined her brother back in the kitchen. "Ready?" Jayson asked her. "Yep," she replied. Jayson said, "Okay on the count of three.

One... Two..." and Rose grabbed her glass and started chugging it. Well, about halfway through her glass, she got an awful taste in her mouth, and the milk didn't feel so good as it hit the bottom of her stomach. She puked curdled milk all over the kitchen. Jayson was laughing so hard, "What's the matter Sissy? Aren't you gonna finish your milk?" You see, what happened that day was that, as his sister was upstairs using the bathroom, Jayson had put every white substance that he could find in the kitchen that wouldn't change the color of the milk in her glass. So, imagine... Sugar, flour, salt, baking soda, baking powder, coffee creamer, mayonnaise, vinegar, etc.... Rose never again would accept a glass of milk from anyone. If she couldn't open the jug and smell it, she wasn't drinking it. It wasn't too much longer after that. Rose's father had quit his job, and her parents could no longer afford to pay the rent, so they were forced to move out.

Unfortunately, there wasn't any money to get another place to live, so they would have to go stay with their mom's friend Lu Ann's sister in her apartment in West Point, Iowa, until they could save the state check for a couple of months to get a place. They were told that they would not be able to bring Sam with them to her apartment, so they had to find him another home. Rose was devastated. Sam was her cat and, sadly, the only friend she had at that time. She cried and cried, but she still had to say goodbye to her beloved cat. Her heart was broken. They gave him to a family that lived out in the country off the highway. How could they just get rid of him so easily? He had been such a good pet. Rose had trouble sleeping for a while, as she had gotten so used to going to sleep to the sound of him purring in her ear.

Chapter 4
Age 5

After a couple of months, they moved into a trailer at the trailer court in West Point, Iowa. This would prove to be the focal point of the terror Rose would live through for many years to come. You see, one night, Rose was lying sleeping in her bed when she started to feel her blankets move. She stirred a little, and it stopped. So, she went back to sleep. All of a sudden, she jumped, wondering why it felt like someone's hand was touching her. Startled, she sits up this time. She couldn't feel anyone now, and it was extremely dark. So, she thought to herself, maybe she was just dreaming so she went back to sleep.

A couple of nights later, as she lay there sleeping again, her blanket felt like it was moving. It startled her, and she jumped. Just like before, though, after she jumped from waking up, she didn't feel it anymore. So, she decided to just lay still and pretend like she was sleeping to see if it happened again or if she was indeed dreaming. She laid very still. All of a sudden, she felt her blanket moving again. And then she felt someone's hands touching her. She continued to lay as still as she could, but she was feeling a little scared. As she looked around her room, there was a slight light shining through the cracked door. She was still trying not to move, so she just moved her head to look around. The light from the door didn't light up the room enough. It was pitch black, besides the tiny glimmer of light through the door. It didn't light up the room enough to see anything. Now, the hand was on her stomach. She was trying so hard to lay still, but she was frightened. "What is touching me," she wondered to herself as she lay there shivering with someone's hand touching her. She was holding her breath. All of a sudden, the hand that had been on her stomach started to move downwards, and was now touching her on her lower abdomen. She was terrified. "Oh no, what is this person doing to me? Are they gonna hurt me? Who is it that is touching me anyway?" She thought to herself as she lay there, not moving, nor breathing, because she was holding her breath. All of a sudden, she jumps, throws her blanket back, and sits straight up in her bed. She still didn't know who was touching her, but what startled her and made her jump up so fast was that the hand that had been moving down her stomach had just slid down the front of her panties and had touched her on her privates.

She was sitting there terrified, wanting to scream, while still not even knowing where this person was. She knew the person was still in her room, because the door hadn't moved at all. She sat there with tears in her eyes, holding her breath, and scared to move. She was trying to listen for this person that was in her room, but all she could hear was her own heartbeat and herself breathing.

She finally laid back down on her bed and curled the blanket around her like a cocoon. She just laid there scared, as she stared at the light through the crack of the door. She was hoping that whoever this person was, that they would just go away, and not touch her anymore. She knew the person still had to be in her room, because her door hadn't moved. As she lay there confused, and terrified, she saw someone's shadow appear where the glimmer of light was from the door, so she strained her eyes to see if she could tell who it was as they moved past her doorway. All of a sudden, she saw the person's face as it passed by the light from the door. It was her oldest brother. "What are you doing?" she asked. "Shhh..." he replied, and then he quickly left her room. She lay there for a little while wondering why he wasn't sleeping and why he was in her room in the dark touching her.

She somehow felt a little better at this point, because at least this person was someone she knew, and wasn't a stranger in her house. However, that didn't change the questions running through her mind. Eventually, she drifted back to sleep.

The next day, she and Jayson were out wandering and just walking around town, trying to find something to do or get into. Rose was with Jayson a lot, because she wasn't allowed to leave the yard unless she was with one of her brothers. Her parents would often say, "Little girls can't be outside by themselves, because bad things can happen to little girls." She would shrug her shoulders whenever they said that, cause she had no idea what they meant by bad things. As the two kids were walking around, they decided to go to the local nursing home. They went there quite a bit, they would visit with the older people, and help them put puzzles together, and even sometimes, they would read books to the older people. Rose really liked going there, but could only go when Jayson wanted to go, since she couldn't go anywhere alone. She always liked tagging along with Jayson, because he would go explore all kinds of fun things. Just like she remembers going to the hog slaughter place close to the trailer court. However, when Jayson would do something that Rose knew he wasn't supposed to do, she would often tattle on him after they got home. Jayson hated when his sister told on him.

You see, by this time, the kids would get spanked when they did something wrong. What sucked was they wouldn't get spanked with a hand; they would get spanked with a belt or with the paddle that Rose's father had made out of a 1x4-inch board. He carved a handle at one end, and wrapped it with duct tape. He then drilled holes through the paddle part of the board to make it sting more when he would spank the children with it.

Rose was finally able to start school that fall, now that she was 5 years old. "She was so excited that she got to go to school with her brothers. And she got to ride the bus, too. She was so excited that she was finally a big girl, a kindergartner. She really liked school. Her class would do fun activities, and they were learning things like how to write their names and the abc's and how to count. And they also got to go to the gym, where they would play with balls, jump ropes, or with this big rainbow-colored parachute. Sometimes, if it was nice outside, they'd go outside for gym class and do something like play kickball, or sometimes they even played tether ball, hopscotch, or even jump rope.

Rose enjoyed playing with her friends with the jump ropes, and she was pretty good at it. As a matter of fact in no time at all, she knew how to twirl the ropes and how to jump really well doing double dutch. She knew exactly when it was safe for her to approach the twirling ropes and start jumping, because she would pay close attention to the sound of the ropes hitting the ground. So, as the back rope hit the ground, that was her cue to jump over the front rope as it started its ascent up and over her head. And then she would jump and jump until it was someone else's turn to jump, or if it was her turn to twirl the ropes. This had to be her favorite thing to do in gym class, or at recess.

Her class also got to go to music class, where they would learn to sing songs. They also have to go to art class and do stuff like color, paint, cut stuff with scissors, or glue stuff. And they even got to play with clay, and make stuff out of messy paper mache.

She was really enjoying school, except for the fact that some of the kids at school were starting to pick on her, and make fun of her, and laugh at her.

They would tell her that her clothes were ugly or that they looked like old people's clothes. They would also tell her that her shoes were ugly, which they kind of were, cause they were old and stained. Rose was sometimes sad because of the things they would say to her, but when she would tell her mom, her mom would just tell her to ignore them.

That was hard to do, cause she just wanted them to be nice to her and to be her friend. Rose was pretty excited the first time it was picture day at school. However, her parents didn't have any money, so they weren't able to pay for any pictures. So, when pictures came back, and the teacher passed them out, most of Rose's classmates would pull pictures out of all different sizes from the large envelopes that they had come in, as well as a class picture. Rose only had a class picture. When she pulled it out of the envelope, one of the boys in her class said, "Your mommy and daddy must be poor cause you didn't get any pictures." "Haha, Rose's parents are poor," he would taunt and tease her. And now he had other kids saying it, too. Rose tried hard just to ignore the other kids teasing her or laughing at her. She just tried to concentrate on her school work and she loved whenever she got a star or a smiley face from the teacher on the top of her papers as the teacher passed them all back out to the children.

She was learning at an exceptional rate, absorbing things like a sponge. Her oldest brother still paid her visits in the middle of the night, but now he was pulling down her panties, and he would kiss her on her privates. And he would make her touch his privates; he would tell her not to tell, or she would get in trouble. What he was doing didn't hurt. It kind of tickled sometimes and she would giggle, and he would always say "Shhh… do you want to get in trouble?"

One night, he did something new, and it hurt when he did it. He stuck his finger inside of her privates. "Ouch," she said, as she yanked his hand off of her. Again, he said to her, "Shhh… someone is gonna hear you, and you're gonna get in trouble." She was starting to think about telling her mom, especially after he hurt her this time, but was afraid of getting spanked, because he had told her she would get in trouble for telling. And even if she had thought of telling her mom if he hurt her. Again, it would have to wait. See, within a couple of days of him hurting her, an ambulance came rushing towards their house with their lights flashing and the horns howling super loud. They steadily just kept getting louder the closer they got. They stopped right in front of the trailer, as two men exited the ambulance, rushed into their home, loaded their mother onto the stretcher, and loaded her into the back of the ambulance. Rose could see blood on her mother's clothes as well as on the sheets that were on the gurney, and that was across her lap. She didn't know what had happened, or why her mother had all that blood on her. She felt sad and scared and hoped that her mom was going to be okay. Her mother was actually hemorrhaging that day, and had to be rushed a hundred miles away to the University of Iowa Hospital to have an emergency surgery, that was called a hysterectomy.

Rose and her brothers had to go to the neighbor's trailer until their mom and Rose's dad were able to return home. The neighbor lady had put pillows and blankets on her living room floor and that was where the kids would sleep.

On about the third night at the neighbor's house, Rose's oldest brother was doing the same stuff to her that he had been doing to her when he would pay these visits to her in the middle of the night. He pulled at her panties, until he finally got them down. He was startled, when he heard the lady whom they were staying with walking, so he quickly laid down and covered up, but he was still touching his sister's privates under the blanket.

Well, as she flipped on the light to check on the children, she saw the blanket moving, and then it quickly stopped. So she pulled the blanket off the children and was shocked when she saw the little girl's panties down and her brother's hand touching his sister's private area. She separated the children by sending Rose in to lie in her bed, while the boys remained in the living room. She then called the 24-hour number for The Department of Human Services and told them what she had just discovered. The following day, a social worker came to the neighbor's house, and it was decided that the oldest brother would be placed in a temporary foster home until their mother was able to come home from the hospital and sort it all out.

About a week and a half later, their mother was finally able to come home. Her oldest son was immediately released to his mother's care. For a while after her oldest brother returned home, Rose wasn't allowed to sleep in her bed, she was made to sleep on her parent's bedroom floor, and if her parents wanted to take a nap during the day, she would have to go lay on their floor, until they woke from their nap. This only lasted for about two weeks, before Rose was sent back to sleep in her bedroom again.

Rose's brother didn't come into her room for about three or four nights. But by the fifth night, Rose wakes to yet once again her oldest brother in her room doing all these things to her, just as before. Well, since she now knew that what he was doing to her was wrong, and that they weren't supposed to be doing them things, she tells her mom the next morning. When she told her mom, her mom's response was "Shhh... we can't talk about that, because those bad people will take you kids away, and we'll never see each other ever again." Since her mother had told her not to talk about it, and since she was scared about being taken away and not seeing her family ever again, she never spoke of it

Chapter 5
Age 6

Time was starting to move fast. Rose was now 6 years old and in the first grade. She really enjoyed learning new things at school. Rose would often get called on by the teacher to answer questions. And she also was the teacher's little helper. So, some of the kids would tease her, calling her teacher's pet.

Rose kept getting sick with tonsillitis, and eventually was told that she was going to have to have surgery to have her tonsils taken out. She was scared about having to stay in the hospital, but the nurses were very nice and made sure that she was comfortable, and had plenty of things to keep her busy. Rose enjoyed reading and coloring, so they made sure she had a lot of books to read and a lot of coloring pages to color.

After surgery, her throat hurt really bad, and she was barely able to swallow. But the nurses told her that she could have as much ice cream and as many popsicles that she would like. She really thought that was pretty cool. She only had to stay two nights and three days, and then she was able to go home. It didn't take long till her throat healed, and she was back to feeling normal.

During the summer following her first-grade year, she remembered that when the town had its annual sweetcorn festival, both of her parents got jobs working for the carnival. Her mother would sell tickets in the ticket booth, and her father would run one of the rides. The kids thought that it was pretty cool that they were allowed to ride all the rides for free and could ride them as many times as they would like.

However, the kids were also instructed by their parents that they were to walk around and pick up any beer or soda bottles or cans that they saw laying on the ground. There was a big bag next to her father on the ride he was operating, where the kids were to put the cans as they picked them up.

The children had gone to the ticket booth to ask their mother if they could get some food or something to drink from the food truck, but they were told that they could eat the free corn and get some water from the drinking fountain, because they didn't have money to buy things like that.

However, the children were sent a few times to buy their parents sodas and even a funnel cake from the food truck.

Rose also remembered that she had ridden the Ferris wheel with Jayson, and when they were at the top of the Ferris wheel, Jayson would rock the seat pretty hard to make her believe that they were gonna tip over. Jayson wasn't really gonna make them flip over, but he sure did like to pick on his sister and make her scream. This would prove to make Rose scared of heights in the future.

By the time Sunday rolled around, Rose's mom had a really bad asthma attack and was taken by ambulance to the hospital in Ft. Madison. Since they didn't have a vehicle, the kids couldn't visit their mother. Rose was always scared when they took her mom by ambulance because sometimes, she would be in the hospital for a long time.

After her mother was hospitalized, Rose learned to cook easy things like scrambled eggs and toast, or macaroni and cheese, and even pot pies. You see, her dad had tried to cook macaroni and cheese for the kids. He put some cold water in a pan, dumped the noodles in the water while it was cold, and cooked them that way. Let's just say they were the starchiest, driest, chewiest noodles the kids had ever eaten. It was immediately decided that they no longer wanted him to cook for them when their mother wasn't there.

As the summer quickly came to an end, it was time for school to begin again. Rose was entering the second grade, and that meant her brothers were in fourth and fifth grade. Within the first month of second grade, Rose was way more advanced than her classmates. In fact, she was doing fourth-grade schoolwork. Rose's teacher had asked her mother to come to the school for a meeting. The teacher explained that Rose was way ahead of her class and had been working on fourth grade schoolwork, and asked her mother's permission to allow them to move Rose to the fourth grade. Rose was so proud and excited that she might be able to get the same grade as Jayson. She hoped that her mother would say yes, but instead, her mother told the teacher that she wanted Rose to stay in the class with children her own age. Rose was really sad, but she couldn't get her mother to agree. When she tried to ask her

Mom if she would please change her mind, her mother said, "I said no, and I mean no." Rose knew that if she brought it up after that, she would be punished.

I bet you're probably wondering by now if her brother was still coming to her room at night. Well, the answer would be yes. Except now things had progressed to oral acts, him sticking his finger inside of her a lot, and he had even tried to kiss her and stick his tongue in her mouth. Yuck!! She hated him coming into her room, but she couldn't stop him, since she wasn't allowed to talk about it. Because if she did, she wouldn't be able to see her family ever again, and that terrified her.

The children always had to walk across the street from the trailer court to wait for the school bus each morning. Rose recalled one morning while waiting for the bus, her oldest brother was climbing on someone's porch, and she knew that he wasn't supposed to be up there, so she said, "If u don't get down, I'm gonna go tell Mom." "You don't have time to go tell her, cause you'll miss the bus," he replied. "Well then, I'm gonna tell her when we get home from school, and you're gonna get in trouble," she said to him. "Haha, you're gonna get in trouble, you're gonna get in trouble," she taunts him. That made him really angry, and he said to her, "If you don't shut up, I'm going to kick you in your mouth." "Good", she replied. "C'mon, right here… right here," she said, pointing at her mouth. He surely did kick her in her mouth with his cowboy boot. He had busted her lip open, and it was instantly bleeding; in fact, the whole front of her was covered in blood. She surely couldn't go to school like that, so she ran home crying holding her mouth.

Mom was very angry at her brother for kicking her in the mouth. She said he was gonna get his ass beat when he got home. "That's what he deserves," she thought to herself. When Rose knew it was about time for the boys to be home, she went into the living room with her mother to wait for them to get there. As soon as they came in the door, she said, "I told Mom what you did."

However, Rose didn't expect what happened next. The boys told their mother that Rose was instigating her oldest brother, and that's why he had kicked her. Her brother didn't get in trouble at all that day. Instead, Rose got her ass beat for instigating her brother. So, with her mouth, bottom, and pride hurt, she ran to her room and cried herself to sleep.

During Labor Day week that year, Rose's parents had decorated three coffee cans for the MDA telethon and made slits in the lid. During the week the kids would be dropped off at different stores, each with a canister. They were told to stand outside the entrance and ask people if they wanted to donate to the MDA. About once an hour, they would come back and empty the kid's canisters. During the week, the children would stand at the store for about four hours, and during the weekend, they were there for 8-10 hours. Rose thought it was pretty cool that she was able to help collect money for these children that suffered from crippling diseases. Little did she know that a couple of years later, she would discover that her parents only turned in the checks and a tiny bit of cash to make it look good.

Yes, she and her brothers were made to do this for at least 5 years. And they weren't really collecting for the MDA so much, they were actually collecting the money for her parents. She was sure that between the three children, they probably collected between 3 and 5 thousand dollars a year. Rose was pretty shocked when she had discovered what they were doing with the money, but the children were told to keep their mouths shut, and that if they told anyone, that they would get their ass beat. She remembered comments from her parents, like well, at least if the children steal, then at least chances were that the police would just give the children a warning, rather than Rose's father going to jail.

Chapter 6
Age 7

On Rose's 7th birthday, she got up and dressed for school, just like any other day. She and her brothers went to stand at the bus stop to wait for the bus. As they got on the bus and took their seats, Rose felt a little sad. Not one single person in her house had told her happy birthday that morning.

However, when the kids got home from school, Rose's dad said to her, "I bet you thought I forgot what today is." "I think it's time for a birthday spanking," he said. He had his paddle ready. He had Rose bend over his knee, and he administered the first swing. "Owww…." she said. "That's one; only six more to go," he said. He really seemed to be enjoying himself, as with each swing of that paddle, he swung a little harder. He hadn't even noticed that his daughter had been in tears since the second swing of that paddle. When he finished, Rose went to her room and with a sore bottom, she laid in her bed and cried herself to sleep. As she woke the next morning, she noticed that her bottom still hurt. When she looked in the mirror, she could see her bottom was bruised. She walked around with bruises for the next couple of weeks.

It was around that time that one morning as the children waited for the school bus, Jayson said to her, "Hey, sissy, I dare you to put your tongue on this pole." "No," she replied. "If I do it, will you?" he asked her. Let's just say that both children regretted their decision almost immediately, because both of their tongues were stuck to the frozen pole. By the time they were both free, they had easily taken a couple of layers off of their tongues. They would never do that again.

Well, as winter quickly turned to spring. It was picture time at school again. Rose's mom had decided to curl her daughter's hair for pictures. Hermom was sitting in a chair at the kitchen table, and Rose sat on the floor between her mom's legs.

As her mom started curling her hair and spraying hair spray, Rose's tummy started hurting. She told her mom that she thought she was going to throw up. So she went to the bathroom, and did indeed throw up. Then she came and sat back between her mother's legs. Her mother started curling her hair and spraying hair spray again when, all of a sudden, Rose went into convulsions. Frantically, her mother told Jayson to go get help. Well, since the town is so small, there's only one cop in town.

Jayson ran as fast as he could to the cop's home and pounded on the door until he answered. "My mom told me to get help," he said. "There's something wrong with my sister."

Rose woke up scared and confused and started crying. She wasn't sure why she was laying on a gurney at the hospital, or how she had gotten there. Last she remembered, her mom was curling her hair. She underwent a lot of testing, and the final diagnosis was that Rose had epilepsy and would have to take anti-seizure medicine. She would also have to be careful not to hit her head too hard and watch climbing on things till the medicine was all the way in her system in about 30 days. She would occasionally have to have the dose of her medicine adjusted as she grew.

on the other side. As she let go of the weight it didn't stay on the bar instead it came straight down, and landed on her toes. In fact, it split her middle toe in half and blew out the side of her second toe.

It just felt tingly until she looked down and saw the blood. She was in tears. Her dad drove her into town to the doctor to have her toes stitched. Rose felt safe with her Daddy there. She loved her Daddy and was still Daddy's girl.

Her toes healed within a couple of weeks. Rose also remembered getting stitches another day while living there. Her mom was going to slap her in the mouth one day for back talking or something.

Well, when her mom went to slap her, she took off running from her mom, cause she didn't want to be hit. Well, her mom had just waxed the floors that day, so as Rose's foot hit a rug, the rug slipped, causing her to fall. When she fell, she split her head open on a radiator heater. Once again, she had to go get stitches. The cut was near her temple on the left side of her face. Her mom was mad that Rose had tried to run away from her that day, so when she returned home from getting stitches, she also got a spanking. With a sore face and bottom, she laid in her bed and cried herself to sleep.

Her oldest brother's visits continued. However, he was now having intercourse with her. She wished that these people would take him away again. She just wanted him to stop doing these things to her. She wished she could talk to someone, but she knew that was forbidden talk.

Her dad had stopped taking care of the farm animals, so they would have to move yet again.

Chapter 7
Age 8

They still lived in the country but at a different farmhouse. This one was about 10 miles from West Point. The landlord lived on the same property. He used to live in the house that her parents were renting, but had built a new house on the property, and decided to rent out the old one, rather than tear it down. Rose was now 8. The landlord actually owned an apple orchard that started on one side of the highway, as well as a bunch of trees that were on the other side of the road, where they also had a little country store.

Rose and Jayson loved feeding the horses apples, because the horses really liked them, and it was just funny to watch the horses drool all over themselves as they enjoyed the apples. However, the landlord also had a couple of bulls. Now, Jayson never took advice from someone warning him about dangerous stuff. He always had to test boundaries or learn for himself. So, one day, as Jayson and Rose were walking down the long driveway after getting off the school bus, Jayson told Rose that he's gonna go piss one of the bulls off and make them chase him. Rose told him he better not, because he's gonna get hurt. Naw, not Jayson. He's invincible, or so he thought. Now he surely did piss the bull off, and that bull surely did chase him. Jayson's calculations were a bit off that day. You see, as he went to jump over the barbed wire fence, he didn't quite make it. Instead of him going over it, he went through it. Maybe not his best decision of the day, cause he was pretty much covered in a bunch of little cuts. Rose told him he was gonna get hurt. Maybe he should have listened to his sister.

One day as Rose had finished eating her food outside, she stood up to go throw her plate away. As she reached across the table to grab her empty paper plate, she got a really bad pain off to the

right side of her neck in the front. The pain was bad enough that Rose was in tears. Her mom told her to rest. Well, it continued to hurt really bad over the next couple of days, so her mom decided that she better go to the hospital. Turns out, her collarbone was broken. How is that possible? She had simply extended her arm forward, and the paper plate was empty. Well, maybe it has something to do with the fact that she and her brothers weren't allowed to drink the milk. If they wanted milk, they had to drink powdered milk, because Rose's father liked to have a glass or two with his dinner, and he liked smashing up saltine crackers in a glass and putting milk in it for a snack. Rose probably had a bit of calcium deficiency. She had to wear an uncomfortable brace that pulled her shoulders backward for about six weeks.

One day, while Jayson was exploring the woods, he brought a timber rattler back in a bucket. As these were dangerous snakes that they had been told to be on the lookout for, the landlord killed it by shooting it with his shotgun. Once again, Jayson didn't like being told what to do, nor did he listen to advice. So that wasn't the last of these snakes he would capture. The landlord would just keep killing them.

There were also stick spiders at this farmhouse, also known as walking sticks. It was strange watching a stick with legs, and it was kind of creepy. Rose was always scared of them. Just like she was scared of something else she discovered while outside one night. You see, she was outside, and it was dark. She looked down at the ground at what looked like a large rock. As she quickly tried to think if there had always been a rock there, the rock hopped a couple of times. She ran back into the house screaming. As Jayson came over to see what his sister was screaming about, he caught sight of the very large toad. Of course, he thought it was cool, so he quickly gathered some supplies because he wanted to trap and keep it. He put the toad in a five-gallon bucket with a large board and cinder block on top of it. There, that should keep him, Jayson thought. However, the next morning, the bucket was tipped over, and the toad was gone. That was a very large toad to have escaped under all that weight.

Now, not only was her oldest brother still paying her visits, but now, two of her cousins had also done bad things to her. What could she do about it though? She had been told previously not to talk about it, and she knew that when her mom said something she meant it.

That summer, as the sweetcorn festival returned to West Point, her parents would yet again go work for the weekend. However, this time, since they didn't have a car, the children would have to walk the 10-mile trek to West Point, and then when the carnival was finished for the night, they would start their 10-mile walk to get back home. Rose always hated the walk back, because there were always a bunch of bats flying around. She was extremely afraid that one of the bats would land on her. Occasionally, they would see an owl on their walk. She was a little scared of the owls as well, but she also thought they looked pretty cool, and liked the noise they made. Before the weekend ended, her mom was once again in the hospital due to her asthma acting up. It was almost starting to seem to Rose that her mother was in the hospital more than she was at home. She was starting to hate the sound of sirens, because they arrived at their home at least two to three times a month.

Within a few months, they would move yet again. This time, to a house in Ft. Madison. It was a yellow house that sat up on two hills. The first step up from the street was way too high for Rose and her mother to step up, so they had put a cinder block in the road to act as another step. The backyard was split-level as well. There was a shed on the hill above the immediate backyard. Let's just say that when it came to mowing this yard, her father had to be creative and tie a rope to the lawnmower. He would let it roll down the hill and then pull it back up using the rope.

Chapter 8
Age 9

Rose turned nine shortly after they moved into this house. At the age of 9, Rose was a very petite little girl. She remembers that the doctor would often tell her mother that she needed to make Rose eat more, because she was underweight. It was around this time, that Rose started smoking cigarettes. One evening she was allowed to go with her brothers to a play at the Junior High School. As they were walking to the school, both of her brothers were smoking a cigarette, so she said to Jayson, "Give me a cigarette". Jayson replied, "Ok, but if you're gonna smoke my cigarettes, you're gonna have to inhale them, cause you're not gonna waste them." "Ok", she replied. "How do I do that?" "Take a drag and then suck it in like this," he answered, as he demonstrated what she needed to do. So, she did just as her brother had shown her. She quickly decided that that wasn't one of her best decisions. She instantly started choking and her stomach was hurting, and she felt extremely dizzy. She ended up throwing up and then needed to sit down until the dizziness improved. Jayson was laughing so hard. "Sissy, are you gonna finish your cigarette?" Before you know it, she was inhaling them cigarettes like she had always been a smoker.

It was in this house that Rose would have to start helping her mother a lot more as her mother was sick a lot more these days. Rose was responsible for doing the dusting and vacuuming and helping her mother with laundry. They didn't have an electric washer and dryer, they had one of the old wringer washers. Rose never got to feed the clothes into the rollers, as it's very easy to get one of your fingers, or even your whole hand pulled into the rollers. Her mom would send the clothes through the rollers from the washing machine, and Rose would guide the clothes down into the rinse water. After swishing them in the rinse water for a short time, her mother would flip the rollers out to the side, and she would then feed the clothes back through the rollers to Rose, where she would make sure that they made it into the basket. And finally, they would take the clothes out and hang them on the clothesline with clothespins for them to dry. After they were dry, they would take them all back down and take them inside to fold and put away. Rose recalls one day her, and her mother were working on laundry when there was a knock at the door. Her mother was almost finished ringing out a load of laundry, so when she heard the knock, she tried to hurry and push the last couple items into the rollers. As she did, a couple of her fingers got caught by the rollers and it literally sucked her whole hand into the machine. She starts yelling at Rose, "Pop it.... Pop it." By now, the rollers were part way up her arm.

Panicked, Rose didn't understand what she meant by "pop it" so she popped it in reverse, wringing her mother's arm and hand back out the other way. Her mother had some damaged nerves and tendons in her hand and arm. Just proving how dangerous one of these machines could be.

When they had moved to this house, they had a social worker that started coming to their house once a week. Thinking back, Rose wasn't sure if she was coming to their house, because her brothers had been getting into some trouble, or if she was there for other reasons. Jayson and this social worker hit it off almost immediately. In fact, they were best buds, and called each other Bro 1 and Bro 2.

When the worker started coming to the house she was working on some goal setting with Rose's mother. They worked on some short-term goals, and when asked about some goals like a year or two out, her mother said she'd like to have a Christmas, and go on a family vacation. So, the social worker was gonna save the money that they came up with to obtain these goals. And so, the savings began. But wait, they didn't have extra money, since they couldn't even barely keep the bills paid. How could they accrue extra money?

Rose's dad had started working at the local landfill, so that would help some. Well just like the job at the steel factory, he wouldn't have this job for long either. So instead, almost every day the kids would be made to get out of the car and walk the ditches to collect cans and bottles to recycle, as well as look through garbage cans at the parks and such.

And whenever it would rain, the kids would have to go with their parents after it got dark, to help their parents catch night crawlers to sell for money. Any means possible to make money.

One day, while Rose and Jayson were walking around town, they went to one of the town's parks. The one that they went to was the one with the water fountain in it. On several occasions, when the two would visit this park, Jayson would climb into the fountain and collect change out of the bottom of the water, and would hand the change off to his sister as his hands would get full. The kids would then use this money to buy candy and soda. On this particular day, Jayson said to Rose, "I go in all the time, it's your turn to go in this time."

Rose resisted a little, but with a little persuasion, she climbed over the gate, and entered the water.

Wouldn't you know after she had handed a couple handfuls of change off to her brother, a police car pulled up. As the officer exits the car, they both instantly know who the officer is. It's "Shotgun

Annie." Great... Rose wasn't quite sure why the town referred to her as that, but she didn't want to find out either. The officer tells Rose that she was gonna have to come with her down to the station. And she asked Jayson to please call their parents. He told her that they don't have a phone, and that their mother was currently in the hospital, but he said he could run home and get Rose's father.

Rose cried the entire time she sat at the station waiting for her father and Jayson to arrive. She knew that there would be an ass whooping that was imminent when they got home, but she didn't care, she was so happy when they came through the door. The officer gave her a lecture and told her father that she believed that Rose was scared enough that she wouldn't do it again, so she wasn't gonna file charges. She was absolutely right, not that she and Jayson wouldn't be back to the fountain, but Rose for sure would never climb over that gate again.

Apparently, on Jayson's way home to get Rose's father that day he had stashed the change that they had retrieved before the officer had shown up. Well on the walk back home, Rose's father made Jayson show him where the money was. He gathered up all the change and put it in his own pocket. And that was the last that they spoke of the money. Rose got her ass beat that day, and not even so much for taking the money, but more so because she had gotten caught.

As the summer ended that year and fall was upon them, Rose recalled that during any downtime that they had that they weren't out can hunting, or at the river while their parents fished. Rose hated having to go fishing. However, one day her mother was yelling at her to stay out of the way while she was casting out her line. Funny enough, Rose wasn't anywhere near her mother. As her mother casted her pole, the line didn't even hit the water. In fact, it wasn't Rose that was in the way, it was her mother. As her mom went to cast out her line. The hook ended up in the back of her mother's head.

They had to go to the emergency room to have it cut out of her head. The nurses even laughed and said that the worm was still on the hook.

Probably the worst part about having to go fishing that they would take the fish home, clean them, and then fry and eat them. Rose hated that when the sunfish and bluegills were cleaned and cooked, that she would have to take the fish's skeleton bones out as she ate them. That always grossed her out. She often would just pick through it enough to be excused from the table.

It was around this time that Rose's mom tried to incorporate the children doing dishes. Well let's just say, when the two boys did dishes and some of them were dirty, they weren't allowed to do dishes any longer. However, that wasn't the case with Rose, when she got some dishes dirty, her mom made her wash every dish in the house.

When Rose asked her mother why her brothers didn't have to do dishes after there was something dirty, but yet she had to wash all the dishes. Her mother responded, "Because you will have a husband and children one day and you will have to cook and clean for them." Rose still didn't think that was fair, her brothers were outside having fun and here she was stuck in the house, but she knew better than to press the issue, because she knew what the consequences would be. One thing Rose could always say about her mom is that her house was always spotless, and it always smelled of fresh PineSol.

Chapter 9
Age 10

With the winter months now in swing, Rose was now 10 years old. They still lived in the same house on the double hill. It was around this time that the family social worker was spending a lot more time around her house than in the past. While Jayson and the social worker had quickly become best buds, it was apparent to Rose that the worker didn't really seem to like her very much. As a matter of fact, the worker would often yell at Rose, or would act like she wasn't even in the room, as she would ignore her and only talk to Jayson.

Sometimes this hurt Rose's feelings, she never quite understood why this woman only liked Jayson. She often had thoughts like "I wonder what is wrong with me that makes people not like me and be mean to me." "Maybe it's because I'm ugly and stupid," she thought to herself. Often when she felt like this, she would sit in her room and cry. In fact, sometimes she would hit her head on the wall really hard, or she would hit herself, while saying, "Stupid Rose, it's your fault everyone hates you, you're so ugly." Occasionally, she would even cut herself on her wrists believing that everyone would be happier if she was dead. But then the fear of not knowing what being dead was like, would generally make the cutting stop, at least until the next time. She got pretty good at hiding the wounds until they healed. She was always scared about getting beat if her parents saw the cuts.

At this stage she tried everything she could to be as good of a daughter as she could, because she hated getting spanked, especially considering spanking always consisted of being hit with objects, such as, boards, belts, fly swatters, twigs, wooden spoons, or whatever else was within arm's reach of her parents.

She recalls that after getting whooped, their parents would then say, "Stop all that crying before I give you something to cry about." She never understood why they said that, because they had already given her something to cry about. The whooping was the reason she was crying. She would hurry and wipe the tears away while trying to stop the sobbing, because she absolutely did not want to be hit anymore. Sometimes while getting whooped, her parents would say, "I only spank you, because I love you." What does that even mean?

Rose recalls some harsher punishments while living in this house. If something in the house had been gotten into, if money was missing from mom's purse, or if something in the house was broken, she and her brothers would be called to the living room. If one of the kids didn't fess up, Rose's dad would use a belt or a board, and he would make the children line up. He would then swat the first child on the ass with whichever item he had chosen to beat their ass with that day. If nobody admitted to it, the first child would be sent to the end of the line and the next child would be swatted, and this would go on until someone admitted fault. Often Rose would admit to whatever it was, even though she truly wasn't guilty, and she'd take the final ass whooping just to get the hits to stop. She recalled her oldest brother being made to sit with his urine saturated underwear on his head with the crotch part of it on his nose, when he would have an accident. She also recalled that sometimes if the children touched something that wasn't theirs, that her parents even burnt their fingers with a lighter. If they talked back, cursed, or lied, their parents wouldn't put dish soap in their mouth, instead they would cut a chunk of soap off of a bar of soap and the children would be made to chew it up and swallow it.

Now, Rose's mother on the other hand, if she was going to hit one of the children, she generally would use whatever was close to her. Which may be a switch if outside, a wooden spoon, or the wire end of the flyswatter. Now when her mother would use the flyswatter, the children would walk around with the welt on the bottom of the flyswatter wherever she had hit them. And u better hope that you didn't put your hand back there, because the welts on your hands would really hurt. If they refused to eat what mom had cooked, it would be put in the fridge and the cold plate would be put in front of them to eat for breakfast, if they still didn't eat it, it would become their next meal, and this would go on till they finally ate what was on the plate.

One day while Rose was 10, she went to the restroom, and was startled to see blood when she wiped. She knew what it was from, as she and her mother had discussed this before. However, she also knew what else came along with starting her period, which was the fact that she could now conceive a child. This thought horrified her, as her oldest brother was still coming into her room in the middle of the night at least a couple times a week.

Oh my God, she thought. What if I get pregnant by my brother? She had to do something to prevent that from happening. So, with her brother's next nightly visit, Rose doubled up her fist and hit herself as hard as she could in her lower abdomen over and over again. In fact, this would become a daily ritual. She figured by doing this that at least if she conceived a baby, she was going to kill it before it had a chance to grow. She knew she didn't want a baby, she was only 10, much less one by her brother.

She really wished she could talk to someone about her fears, but she knew if she did, there would be consequences. Why won't he just stop, she thought to herself. Over the next couple

months, Rose developed breasts and started putting on weight rapidly. In just a couple months, she had gone from being extremely small and petite to being overweight with big boobs. And so, the tormenting at school continued. Now she was being told that she stuffed her bra, and of course being called fat. She really wished they would just be nice to her. The teasing really was starting to wear on her. It was starting to make going to school miserable.

As the year progressed, the can hunting and catching nightcrawlers continued. Rose longed for a day where she could just play and be a kid like the other children she always saw playing and laughing and running around.

Since Rose's mom was in the hospital more these days, she and Jayson would occasionally go to the social worker's house. One day when the worker brought the children back home, she and Jayson had decided that they were gonna tell their mother that Rose had done all kinds of bad things at her house. Rose indeed had not done any of the things she was accused of, but that's exactly how things played out when they arrived home. So, Rose's mother stood up, with her wire flyswatter in her hand. All of a sudden, Rose feels the burn of the wire end of the flyswatter across her lower back, as she heard her mother say, "Is this what you guys want? Huh?

Does this make you happy? Is this what you want?" as she continues to hit Rose. Rose probably was hit about 25 times that day… across her back, her bottom, her hands, arms, and legs. Now what's so messed up about this whole situation, was that this was a social worker, employed by the state of Iowa to protect children. Now, not only had this social worker made up lies to instigate the situation, but she also stood there and watched Rose's mother beat her with that flyswatter. She made no attempt to try to stop her mother, she just watched. Rose went to her room, where she cried herself to sleep.

With summer in full swing, so was lots of can hunting, worm catching, and fishing trips. During the summer, a couple of Rose's cousins had come to spend a couple weeks. However, by the time her cousins returned home, Rose had now officially been molested by four of her cousins. She really wanted all of it to stop, including her oldest brother's frequent nightly visits. She wanted to talk to someone, but who?

As July neared the end, the children were told that they were going to be going on vacation to St Louis. The kids were pretty excited, because they had never been on vacation before. The trip was planned for the first week of August, which meant Jayson would be turning 12, while they were there. On this birthday, Jayson received gifts. As a matter of fact, he had at least 10 presents. All of the countless hours that the kids spent walking ditches, was finally paying for something. While they were there, they went to the caverns, the zoo, the brewery, and the arch. And they also got to eat at White Castle.

They all enjoyed spending an entire day at the zoo, however, there were areas of the zoo that all of them had missed. Oh well, maybe they'd get another chance in their life to visit St. louis. The brewery was fun, after a tour, everyone entered a bar area. Adults were allowed to drink as much beer as they'd like for 15 minutes, the soda machines were free for 15 minutes also. Of course, Rose's parents made the children keep getting cans of soda out of the machine till the social worker and her mother's purse were completely full of cans of soda. Now at the Arch, Rose's mother and oldest brother said immediately that neither of them had any desire to go to the top.

Rose's father and Jayson said they for sure were going up. Rose was feeling a bit scared since she had seen how high it was up in the sky on their way in. But of course, whatever Jayson did, Rose was right behind him. This was a decision she would soon regret. First, they were in this cramped little egg shaped elevator that twitched back and forth till it finally reached the top. Rose's father and Jayson instantly walked directly out and straight to look out the windows. However, that was not the case for Rose. The minute she stepped off the elevator she could feel the slight movement of the top of the arch. Instantly it made her lightheaded, her legs were shaky, and she was sick to her stomach. In fact, she crawled all the way across the top of that arch on her hands and knees until she got to the other side. Guaranteed, not a decision she would ever make again.

Before they knew it the week was up, and they were back in Ft. Madison, back to doing all the things that Rose was really starting to resent. She didn't want to walk the ditches after school, she wanted to go play like other kids did. She didn't want to stand outside a store for a week holding a canister collecting money for the MDA, since she now knew the truth behind her and her brothers again working for their parents. I mean, if they wanted to steal the money, why couldn't they themselves stand there and collect the money? Oh that's right, cause ppl would donate more if a cute little kid was asking.

Fall quickly turned to winter. The kids, well into the winter, were still made to walk the ditches, except with coats, hats, and gloves for them, since the only thing that stopped them having to walk the ditches, is when it finally snowed enough that the ditches were buried with snow.

One day, when Jayson and Rose were at the social worker's house, they decided to look through the worker's closets. When they did, they discovered a whole bunch of toys, and they told each other what they had each seen. Those had to be gifts for them, since that's what else the worker was saving money for. Once Rose's mom learned that they knew what they were getting for Christmas, she took the gifts back to the store. She did, however, buy them different gifts.

On Christmas morning, the kids were all called to the living room by their mother. Next thing you know, you hear bells ringing and someone saying Ho Ho Ho! Their mother tried to play it off trying to convince the children it was Santa rather than Rose's father in the suit. Come on, the children were now 10,12, and 13, they obviously knew there wasn't a Santa, since this was their first celebrated Christmas. Rose's father (Santa), Started with her oldest brother and said he had to go see if there were presents on his sleigh for the children.

Granite the kids knew that when he said sleigh, that just meant in the kitchen. So, he re-enters the living room with a bike box that contained a ten-speed bicycle that had to be assembled for her oldest brother. Next, he leaves the room and comes back with a five speed in a box, this one intended for Rose. Then he says to Jayson, "Let me go see if Santa has anything for Jayson." When he came back to the room, he said, "Sorry Jayson, Santa doesn't have anything for you on his sled today. I guess you've been a bad boy this year." So, he sat down for a couple minutes, and then said, "Let me go check one more time." And that's when he brought in Jayson's box with his BMX type bike.

For some reason, Rose thinks she may remember Jayson crying that morning, because of the little prank about Santa not having a gift for him.

After the bike ordeal, they went back to opening gifts like any other family. Of the gifts exchanged that morning, the ones that stood out for Rose, were as follows. She recalled that the main gift that her oldest brother had received was an electric guitar and amplifier. Jayson got a remote control car and multiple pairs and colors of parachute pants. There were red with black zippers, black with red, gray and black, solid black, and there may have even been black with blue zippers. Rose's gifts that stood out that year were a cabbage patch, and a doll lamp with a beautiful blue dress.

She recalled that she and her brothers had gotten their Mother a large set of chimes that year as well as a microwave (that they soon discovered would be moving on to a new home, cause their mother was just not down with using a microwave). She recalls for her father they had bought him a pocket watch. Her parents had gotten a new wedding set that year, which resembled Jesus' crown. Jayson and the social worker had gotten matching bracelets that said Bro1 and Bro2.

Now the craziest gift that she recalls from that year, was for her father, since his birthday was also on Christmas Day.

This was a gift from the social worker, and was a bit of a gag gift. She had given him a condom filled with water on a chain, so it was basically a necklace. A bit of a strange gift, I mean since this was the family's worker from social services. It was however a good Christmas, and Rose was so excited about wearing new clothes to school after the winter break was over. Even just for one time, it was nice to go to school in nice clothes.

Within a couple weeks all the kids' bikes were put together. Not that they could even ride them, since it was wintertime.

It was around this time that Rose and Jayson again went to the social worker's house for a couple days. During this visit, the worker and Jayson were up to their usual shenanigans. At that time, the cable boxes for the televisions had a rotary dial on the front. Well, whenever Rose was told she could watch what she wanted for a little while, she would grab the dial and spin it to the channel she wanted to watch. Every time she would spin the dial like that, the worker would yell at her. Normally when the worker yelled at her, Rose would start crying, put on her shoes and coat and would run outside wanting to go home. However, this time when Rose opened the door to the coat closet to grab her belongings, she saw something that made her collapse to the floor sobbing hysterically. When she opened that door, what she saw was her cabbage patch doll hanging on a noose. She was beyond upset at this point and grabbed her shoes out of the bottom of the closet.

She noticed immediately that her shoes were stuffed full of spaghetti. She then stands up and yanks her coat from the hanger. As she tries to put on her coat, she finds that the sleeves of her coat were completely filled with clothes. She ran outside into the snow with just socks on her feet.

For a short time, Jayson and the worker locked the door and wouldn't let her in as they sat inside laughing at her. These were some extremely cruel tricks for the worker to engage in.

Chapter 10
Age 11

With a new year just starting off, Rose turned 11. Still at the yellow house at that point. Her mother's health kept deteriorating, and the nightly visits from her oldest brother continued. She continued punching herself everyday as hard as she could in her lower abdomen, in fear of conceiving her brother's child, and she still spent a lot of time in her room, as again, she wasn't allowed outside where bad things happen to little girls.

Rose spent a lot of time listening to music those days. As a matter of fact, it was around that time, she heard a song on the radio that would soon become the theme of her life and give her the strength to keep going. The song was titled, *"Greatest Love of All"* by Whitney Houston. The lyrics of this song were so powerful, it was almost as if Whitney Houston had written the song with what Rose was going through in mind. The song began as....

"I believe the children are our future, teach them well and let them lead the way.

Show them all the beauty they possess inside. Give them a sense of pride to make it easier.

Let the children's laughter, remind us how we used to be."

Now the next two sets of lyrics would be where the song totally catches Rose's attention...

"Everybody searching for a hero.

People need someone to look up to. I never found anyone who fulfilled my needs. A lonely place to be, so I learned to depend on me.... I decided long ago, never to walk in anyone's shadow. If I fail, if I succeed, At least I live as I believe.

No matter what they take from me, they can't take away my dignity".

Then the chorus begins......

"Because the greatest love of all is happening to me, learning to love yourself that is the greatest love of all."

She was so right with these lyrics. No matter what kept being taken from Rose, they couldn't take her dignity. While she wished that her brother would stop having sex with her, and that she didn't have to punch herself every day, it was just what she had to deal with.

Jayson had started riding his bike even though there were several inches of snow on the ground. Rose and their oldest brother were holding off until closer to spring to ride theirs. Well one day around February, her dad needed a part for his car in order to make it run again. Since he didn't have a ride to go across town to get the part, he decided that he would ride his daughter's bike to go get what he needed. Well, when he returned home, he was pushing the bike instead of riding it. You see, what had happened, was that apparently he had at some point, decided to stand up while pedaling.

When he did, with him being a large man, he snapped the right pedal completely off. He promised that he would get it fixed soon, but that wasn't the case.

Soon thereafter, they moved yet again. This time to a house across town about a block from Aunt LuAnn's house. One nice afternoon, with her mother in the hospital again, Rose's father decided they were gonna go to Aunt LuAnn's to visit. When they got there, Aunt LuAnn had told Rose that the twins were out back playing. So, Rose went to join the boys out back. Well, they were in the alley with a dirt bike, and they'd ride as fast as they could to the other end of the alley and then lock up the brakes and skid out. Rose was looking pretty good the first couple of times she did it, but then something horrible happened. Rose and the bike basically had taken on the formation equivalent to that of a pretzel. She couldn't move. She was in an awful lot of pain and crying by now. Her dad had to come pick her up and carry her to his car, and they were on their way to the hospital.

As one could imagine with any mother, as soon as her mother learned that her daughter was in the ER injured, she wanted to get out of bed and go downstairs immediately. Well, the nurses had a bit of a fight on their hands trying to keep her in her bed. She had oxygen on and was hooked up to a few different IVs. Now, by the time her mother was about to start yanking out her wires, they had received word from the ER that they were indeed admitting Rose. It turned out she had broken her left leg, ankle, and the growth plate in her foot. She didn't actually have to have surgery on her foot, but they were still going to take her to the operating room and put her to sleep in the morning, so they could reset her foot and ankle as they cast it.

Now, normally there was a floor for children separated from the adults, however since mom was so worked up and daughter was scared about staying in the hospital, they decided to make special accommodations for the night and allow Rose to stay in the room with her mother.

Rose woke a couple of times in the middle of the night crying in pain, and her mother was quick to alert the nurses that she needed more pain meds. Just as Rose got into a really good sleep, the nurses came in to give her meds to put her asleep for the OR. Now, by the time Rose was wheeled back in from the recovery room, her mother had been discharged. They said that Rose would have to stay till the next morning, so that she could be fitted for crutches, and physical therapy could work with her to get her used to using the crutches. Rose didn't want to stay by herself, but the day flew by as she just slept a lot due to the pain meds keeping her kind of sedated. The following day, she went home with her crutches. Within a couple of days, Jayson decided to kick her crutch and make her fall. She smacked her cast foot against the sidewalk. Jayson then said, "Sorry, I didn't see you there."

The school year wrapped up, and Rose's foot had healed enough to get her cast off. One day, as Jayson and Rose were upstairs in Rose's room, sitting on her bed, which was parallel between the window and the door, they were both smoking a cigarette. Apparently, her father had decided to sneak upstairs because he thought it seemed too quiet up there. Well, as he approached the doorway of her room, he could see that Jayson had a lit cigarette. Jayson was sitting on the side of the bed closest to the door. "Put it out," he says. Rose, startled by the sound of her father's voice, also quickly put out her cigarette. "Oh, you too huh?" he asked. You see, when he approached the doorway, he had only seen Jayson's cigarette, since Rose was sitting on the backside of her bed with her hand not visible from the doorway. Damn, she thought to herself. She could have gotten away with it had she just dropped her cigarette on the floor and stepped on it. Too late for that now.

"Get downstairs," her father said. Well, Rose knew what this meant for her, as she had already witnessed both of her brothers go through the same thing in the past. It meant that her father was gonna have a little pow-wow with her. You see, his philosophy was that if he made the children smoke until they threw up that it would make them stop smoking. So, she's made to sit on the floor in front of her father, as he lights a Marlboro red cigarette and hands it to her, and tells her that he wants her to smoke it down to the filter, and that he wants her to inhale every drag. She was made to smoke an entire pack. Next, he lit a non-filter cigarette that she had to smoke till it was burning her fingers.

Lastly, he loaded his tobacco pipe and made her inhale each drag of that till it was empty. The pipe finally made her throw up. However, just like with both of her brothers, it didn't stop her from continuing to smoke either.

One day, while the parents were gone, and Jayson and Rose went walking around town, their oldest brother had decided to bring a much older woman into the house and had sex with her in their parent's bed. Now, the problem was that this woman was on her period, and they made a mess all over the sheets. Instead of trying to change sheets to cover up his actions, he simply threw the blanket over the top of it. Imagine what a surprise it was when their parents went in to go to bed that night. When questioned about it, her oldest brother denied it and told his mother that it must be from her. He must have forgotten that his mother had a hysterectomy six years prior.

On another night, one of the kid's friends from down the road had snuck into the house, because Jayson had left the door unlocked for him. Well, he must have made too much noise coming upstairs cause all of a sudden, the light to the staircase came on, as Rose's dad said, "Hey, what are you guys doing up there? The friend immediately darts under one of the boys' beds. Well, her father checked upstairs and didn't find anything out of the ordinary, but told the kids to get downstairs until he could figure out what they were up to. The kids all came downstairs and were sitting on the couch, relieved that he hadn't seen the friend. All of a sudden, her father stands back up and says, "Wait a minute." He then heads back upstairs, and the kids hear a loud bang accompanied by the sound of her father's voice saying, "Get your ass downstairs." Damn, they were busted. You see, when he had come upstairs the first time, he had looked under the beds and such, but it wasn't until he sat downstairs for a couple of minutes that he realized that he had seen a pair of shoes under one of the boys' beds. After he sat for a couple of minutes, it registered to him that the pair of shoes he saw were straight up and down, instead of being flat on the floor. The kid was sent home as Rose and her brothers got their asses beaten with a belt and sent back to bed.

After the incident with that boy, Rose's bedroom was moved down to the main level to the little room at the bottom of the stairs. Well, as the bathroom was right off of her room, Rose would often use the restroom in the middle of the night without turning on the light. One night, as she was using the restroom, she heard water splashing in the bathtub. It startled her so badly that she jumped up and turned the light on. Now, she didn't know what she expected to see, but there was a catfish in the bathtub that was the entire tub length. Apparently, her parents had caught it while fishing. Let's say they never did end up cleaning that fish to eat, instead, the fish ended up dying and was crammed in a five-gallon bucket and put out to the trash. Rose didn't understand why they didn't let it go if they weren't going to clean it.

Not too much longer after that, Rose's mom had let yet another one of her cousins come to stay with them. He was 24 years old and had just gotten out of the Army. The following day, Rose was looking for Jayson, but she couldn't find him anywhere else in the house, so she decided to look in the basement. Well, that's where she found both of her brothers and their cousin. They were all smoking something that had a funny smell to it. "What's that?" she asked. "Here, take a drag of it," Jayson said. Well, as soon as she did, she blew it right back out cause it made her cough and cough. She had just smoked her first hit of marijuana. The kids were all pretty high and munched on a bunch of food and laughed a lot.

That night, as Rose lay in bed asleep, she was startled awake because there was a hand covering her mouth, and she couldn't move. There was another hand forcing her panties down, as a knee forced her legs apart. She tried to wiggle free, but she couldn't get him off, cause he was too heavy. He forced himself inside her while keeping his hand over her mouth and whispering threats in her ear. He was so large, as he was a grown man, and she was an 11-year-old little girl. He eventually finished, and continued threatening her. She was in so much pain, and when she went to the bathroom, she realized she was bleeding. She lay back in her bed and sobbed till she finally went back to sleep. The next day, she was fairly quiet and withdrawn. As she thought about what happened the night before, the thought of what if she was pregnant now. She knew not to say anything to her mom, because it's not like she'd care anyway after all these years. Every time she used the restroom for about the next week, she would punch herself over and over again, even though her abdomen was still sore from him forcing himself inside her. It was by far the worst experience she ever had. This now brought the cousin count to five.

He left their home a couple days later. Guess he had accomplished what he had come there to do. As summer was wrapping up and the school year was near, Rose recalled that their mother made them sell their bikes in order to get school supplies. Rose never did get to ride her bike since the pedal never got fixed.

One day, while everyone was getting ready to leave the house, their mother kept calling for Jayson. She knew that he had not gone anywhere and was still in the house somewhere. She told her husband to go look in the basement. It appeared that's exactly where he was, however, he wasn't super responsive and was looking a bit discolored. Turned out he had been down there huffing gas fumes out of the gas can to get high. He became fairly combative and aggressive. Turned out Aunt LuAnn came over, and they basically hog-tied him, put him in the back seat, and drove him to Cromwell in Independence, Iowa, where they committed him for drug treatment.

Shortly after school started for the year, Rose's parents had gone with her aunt and uncle to the old threshers and settlers reunion. Within a couple of hours of them being there, her mother was rushed once again by ambulance. Her mother was allergic to basically everything at that reunion. She again, was considered on her deathbed. One of Rose's aunts had even flown in from Washington. The kids and her father began staying at another Aunt's house. Her mother recovered again and was released from the hospital. They ended up getting a small upstairs apartment back in Cedar Rapids.

They stayed only a couple of months before moving into a house across the street from a dairy factory.

The layout of this house was as such, when you walk in the front door, that's the living room. If you walk straight through the living room, you're in the kitchen. To the left of the kitchen was the bathroom, and on the other side of the bathroom was the parent's room. Also, off the living room was a staircase, and at the top of the stairs, there was a room on the left and the right. Rose got the room to the right since it was smaller. The first time Rose closed her door, she realized there was a hook lock and a sliding lock on the inside. Finally, Rose had protection. She could finally prevent her brother’s late-night visits. The first time she locked that door was so liberating, and she promised herself never again. And she meant every bit of that.

Chapter 11
Age 12

As the school year was in full swing, winter had also arrived. Which meant that Rose was now turning 12. She was enjoying the new house and her ability to keep herself safe from late-night visits. Apparently, her oldest brother wasn't enjoying the locks on her door as much as she was. Some nights, she would hear him lightly knocking on her door. "Rose, unlock your door," he would whisper. She would just lay in her bed and act like she didn't even hear him. One night, as she was laying in her bed reading, she heard a rustling noise coming from the door. As she looks over, she can see that some papers are being slid through the crack under the door. She sat still until the paper stopped moving. When she went and picked it up, and unfolded it. Inside, there were a couple of photos that had obviously been torn out of a dirty magazine. The pictures were of people in different sexual positions. On the piece of paper there was a note written on it. It said, "Rose, leave your door unlocked tonight. I want us to do this." She immediately took the note and pictures down to her mom. Her mother simply said, "I'll talk to him." Well, let's just clarify that never happened.

Rose's mom was going to bingo a lot these days. She seemed to be enjoying being around her mom and sisters more. Well, one night, her mom was at bingo with her grandmother, Jayson was still in Cromwell, and her oldest brother was out running around. That left Rose and her dad at home. She never minded being at home with him, cause she was Daddy's girl.

As they were just relaxing watching tv, and Rose was messing around with a yo-yo, her dad asked her if she would go get his pajama pants and underwear, so he could take a bath. So, she got up and went in to get his clothes out for him. As she entered her parent's room, she sat her yo-yo on the bed. She gathered his stuff out of the drawer, and as she turned back towards the bed, she jumped as her father had startled her. She hadn't even heard him come into the room. "You scared me," she said. "I didn't hear you come in. Here's your clothes," she said as she sat them on the bed. She went to grab her yo-yo, which he had picked up when he came in. In fact, he was laying across the bed on his stomach. As she reached for it, he closed his hand. She giggles a little. "Give me my yo-yo," she said as she reached for it again. He again closes his hand. "Dad, c'mon," she says again. He opens his hand and allows her to take it this time. As she turned to leave the room, he said, "Hey, Sissy, if I ask you a question, do you promise not to tell your mom?" "Yes," she said. "Are you sure?" he asked again. "Of course," she replied. She was thinking maybe he was gonna do something nice for her mother, or buy her something. She never could have prepared herself for what he asked her next.

"Do you wanna fool around?" he asked. She froze. Her mind is racing. She's trembling, and tears were stinging her eyes. "Did he just ask me that? He couldn't have, that's my daddy," she said to herself in her mind. She literally just stood there staring at the floor. Shaking her head, no, her whole body was shaking; she was nauseated and felt dizzy. "Oh my god." she thought. "Is he gonna hurt me? I just want to run."

The thoughts were rolling so fast, she felt like she was gonna pass out. It seemed like an eternity that she had been standing. It was almost as if the whole world had just stopped at that very moment.

"Are you okay?" he finally asked. She was still standing there, unable to move. She tried to speak, but no words came out. She lightly nods her head. Her thoughts were, "No, I'm not ok; my father just asked to have sex with me; how can I possibly be ok?" "Now remember, you promised," he said. She just kept looking down, slowly nodding as she made her way to the door. As she cut through the bathroom, she couldn't hold them back anymore. The tears were streaming now; she felt like she couldn't breathe. She made it to the living room as she heard the bathroom door close.

As soon as the door closes, without a moment's hesitation, she grabbed a couple of cigarettes out of her dad's pack, slipped on her shoes, and darted out the door. She ran as fast as she could two blocks down the alley where her cousin lived.

She was sobbing as she pounded on the door. "Please answer," she thought to herself. She pounded again. Still no answer. So, she ran across the street to the gas station and asked a stranger if she could please have a quarter. The person could visibly see how upset she was. "Of course, here," he said as he handed her a quarter. "Hey, are you okay?" he asked. She didn't pause for one second to respond. She simply yelled back through the sobs, "Thank you."

She ran as fast as she could, about six blocks, until she reached a pay phone up under the interstate. Her legs felt like jello, and she was trying to catch her breath as she put the quarter into the payphone and dialed her Aunt's phone number. The phone rang about three times, and then finally her Aunt's voice, "Hello." Rose starts sobbing again as she asks her aunt, "Will you meet me at Peoples Bank, please? And please, please don't tell my dad where I'm at.. "Rose, are you okay?" "Please, will you come get me?" "Yes, I'm on my way," her aunt replied. "Do you promise you won't tell my dad? He can't know where I am. Please promise you won't tell him," she sobbed again. "I promise." "Okay, please hurry."

She slammed down the phone and took off running as fast as she could again, till she got a huge pain in her side, she thought she might faint. She slowed down to walking as she waited for the cramp to go away. All of a sudden, she heard something that stopped her in her tracks, "Rose Anne, what the hell are you doing?" Oh no, her father had caught up with her. She was standing there again, frozen, looking at the ground sobbing, shaking her head no. "How did he catch up with me?" she thought to herself. "I thought he was taking a bath. Now I'm really in trouble, and he's mad. Mom won't be home for a long time still." Her mind is racing. He grabs her by the top of her arm and shoves her in the direction of home. "Get your ass going," he said. As he marched his daughter back towards the house, he said to her, "I swear to god, if you tell anyone, I'll break every bone in your body." She believed that he could. He was 6'3" and probably a solid 300 lbs. He definitely was big enough that he could hurt her pretty easily.

When they reached the house, he said, "Get your ass in the house, and remember what I said." She still just stood there staring at the floor, nodding her head. She couldn't sit down, even though her legs felt like they might collapse under her. "Now I'm taking my bath. And your ass better be out here when I'm finished. Do you understand me?" he asked in an angry voice. She just kept staring at the floor nodding, trying to get the tears to stop.

Her father re-enters the living room after about ten minutes. She hadn't moved. She couldn't move. "Sit your ass down, and stop all that," he said. She kept nodding. She can't move. It's almost as if she's frozen.

All of a sudden, the front door flies open, and her mother enters the house. "What did you do to your daughter?" she asked her husband. "I didn't touch her," He replied. "Tell me, what did you do to your daughter?" she asked again. "I didn't touch her," he responded again. "Rose, what the hell did your father do to you?" she asked her daughter. "I'm not saying anything in front of this man who just threatened my life," she thought to herself, as she was still just standing there staring at the floor, shaking her head.

Her mother grabbed her arm and pulled her outside. "Rose, what did your father do to you?" She started sobbing again as she told her mom what had happened. Her mom then looked at her grandmother, who was still sitting in her car, and said, "Take her to your house; I'll call you in a little while."

Later that night, when her grandmother took her back home, her mother said, "Your dad is in the hospital getting help. I'm going to bed, and you need to, as well." So, Rose went up to her room, locked her door, and cried herself to sleep.

Rose stayed in her room most of the following day. Eventually, her mom yelled upstairs to tell Rose and her oldest brother, who was in his room, to come down for dinner. After the kids sat down and started to eat, her father walked into the room. He took his place at the table and glared at his daughter as he started loading his plate with food.

Rose wasn't hungry anymore. In fact, she was struggling to not throw up. She excused herself from the table, scraped her plate into the trash can, ran up to her room, and locked her door. She lay in her bed, scared, confused, and sad, as she started sobbing again. She must have been drained from the last two days that she had, cause she was probably asleep in less than five minutes. By the next day, it was almost if none of it had even happened, as her parents continued on like normal.

Rose was so happy a couple of days later when her mom yelled upstairs and asked if she wanted to say hi to Jayson while he was on the phone. She needed more than anything to talk to her brother.

As she quietly told Jayson what had happened, Jayson said, "Fuck that, Sissy, I'm running away from this place, and I swear to god I'm coming home to kill your father." "No, Jayson," she pleads.

"Please don't run away Jayson, they'll catch you,and then they'll make you stay longer. I'm ok,

Please just stay there. I love you."

Well Jayson surely did run away from Cromwell, and of course, the staff found him, just like his sister had warned.

Rose started the 8th grade year at Roosevelt Middle School that fall while at this residence.

Chapter 12
Age 13

As winter came around again, Rose turned 13.

Whenever she wasn't at school, she just sat alone in her room, safe from her oldest brother and father. It was during that fall that they moved again to their next residence across town. Rose transferred from Roosevelt to McKinley. Over the years, she had switched schools so many times that she didn't even attempt to make friends anymore. At the new house, Rose didn't have the protection for herself that she did at the last house. In fact,

Rose's room didn't even have a door at this house. After the first time that her oldest brother paid her another late-night visit at that residence, she made the decision that she was going to run away.

One night, after her parents had gone to bed, she took the bag that she had packed and made her escape. Once she was outside in the dark of the night, she almost considered going back.

She was scared. She didn't know where she would go, what she would eat, or where she would sleep. All she knew was that wherever she ended up, it had to be better than where she was and what she had lived through.

Within about a half hour of leaving her house, she ran into one of Jayson's friends. This friend had told her that she could come to stay with her.

After at her place, she said to Rose, "Let's get dressed up and go out." So, they started the whole process of picking out outfits and putting on make-up. Once they were finished, they walked to a BP gas station on First Avenue. The gas station has a door on both sides of the building. The girls were deciding what they wanted to drink when the other girl said, "My dad will be here to get us soon."

Rose thought to herself, "Her dad? Why is her dad coming to get us?" Then reality hit. Now Rose knew that this girl's dad was a well-known pimp in town and that he sometimes would even pimp out his own daughter. She remembered stories that Jayson had told her about this girl. At that moment, she waited for the other girl to start looking around the store again, and she took off running out of the opposite door. She ran as fast and as far away from there, until she couldn't run anymore.

She ended up hiding in some bushes in an alley for at least an hour or better. And then she just went to the park and hid on the equipment to stay out of sight until the sun came up the next day. For the next couple weeks, she stayed with other people she knew off and on.

One day, a Cedar Rapids police officer stopped her and told her that she needed to go back home. "I'm not going back there," she told him. When he asked her why, she said, "Because I don't have a bedroom door." "Well, what does that mean?" he asked. And she told him. For the first time in 13 years, she told someone the whole truth of the nightmare that she had lived up till then. As the words of her mother still played in the back of her mind. "Shhh, we can't talk about that. The state will take you away, and we'll never see each other again." At this time, that was just a risk Rose had to take. Rose was admitted to the psych ward at St.

Luke's hospital, due to lack of a better, safer place to put her, while they got the Department of Human Services involved with the family. In fact, the juvenile psych ward was full, so Rose was put in the adult unit.

Two days before Christmas 1987, Rose was transferred to a foster home. Her foster mom's name was Barb. She was a single mother of a ten-year-old daughter. After Rose was shown where she would be sleeping, she and Barb sat down at the kitchen table to talk for a little while. Barb asked Rose if she smoked cigarettes, and she confirmed that she did. Barb said, "Okay, well, let's go to the store and buy you some." They drove down the block to the gas station, and Barb bought her a carton of Marlboro Reds. After the car ride to and from the store, Rose kind of thought this lady was a bit silly. She was jamming, dancing, snapping her fingers, and singing away to a Gregory Abbott cassette she was listening to. In fact, this was the album that Barb most frequently played when they were in the car. Since Rose really didn't have any clothes, Barb took her into her bedroom, showed her which clothes in her closet were off limits, but told her to pick out a couple of outfits. And she said that she would take Rose shopping for clothes after the holiday.

On Christmas morning, when Barb and the girls awoke, they all met in the living room to open gifts. Now, Rose didn't expect any gifts, as that was what she was accustomed to. Much to her surprise, she had just as many gifts as Barb's daughter had. She thanked Barb for the gifts, in a very humble way.

The day after Christmas, she and Barb went clothing shopping. Barb had her try clothes on to make sure they fit and even offered suggestions of clothes that were better for her size, and that would make her look slimmer. Rose had never experienced this before, and she had a $250 budget to work with. It felt really nice to have new and pretty new clothes.

As the winter break from school ended, Rose started her first day at Prairie Middle School. She was still in the 7th grade. Pretty much from day one, kids started tormenting her about her weight. As she would walk down the hall, they would say, "Boom, boom, boom, save the whales." Rose always believed that had these kids known what she had been through in her life up to that point, that maybe they wouldn't have treated her that way. And who knows, maybe some of them probably still would have.

Chapter 13
Age 14

As it's was January again, and with winter break over, Rose was turning 14. However, this would be a birthday that she had never experienced before. Barb's whole family came over, and they all brought gifts, and there was food , cake, and ice cream. Barb permed Rose's hair for her birthday. There were no birthday spankings. It was just fun. All of Barb's family treated Rose as if she had always been a member of their family.

She had an amazing day. A birthday she would remember for the rest of her days.

Around the time of her birthday, The Children's Home of Cedar Rapids had contacted Barb, and told her that Rose had been chosen among other children that were in foster care and some of the children from the cottages to go to Colorado to climb and camp in the Rocky Mountains. Rose was so excited to go to a different state, and to actually see mountains. She talked about it all the time over the next couple of months.

Jayson had, at some point, gotten out of Cromwell and went to the Wendell house in Cedar Rapids, which was a chance for him to show the state that he could live out of the institution. He wasn't there long until he was then taken to Eldora, which is the state training school for boys.

Occasionally, Rose and Jayson would get to have a conversation over the phone. But most of their communication those days was in writing letters back and forth. Regardless, they always stayed in contact.

It wasn't until around summer that Rose started getting overnight and weekend visits at home with her parents. Rose's first weekend home, her father, mother, and her mother's best friend and children all went to the Cedar Rapids Reds baseball game. It was a little strange that her father paid the extra for her mother to sit in the box seat, while he sat in the bleachers with her friend. She didn't comment, but she definitely observed.

After the game, when they all arrived back home, Rose's mother asked her husband if he and her friend had been messing around. He confirmed that they had. And he said that he was gonna go be with her because she was pregnant. She wasn't pregnant, but that's what she said, so that he'd stay with her, instead of going back to his wife. And this friend of her mother lived just one block down the alley. The following day, her mother sent Rose with a note to go give her father. She was asking him to come talk. So he did. Rose asked her dad a few questions, and he kept responding with "I don't know." Eventually, her mom asked her husband if she could talk to him inside for a minute. Now

Rose wasn't quite sure what had just happened inside, but her dad came flying out the door, off the porch, and down the alley.

Apparently, she had asked him something, and he responded with "I don't know" again. Her mother didn't like his answer, so she grabbed her husband's beard and banged his head against the wall. Her mother, at that time, had beautiful, long, natural nails that were all about an inch long over her fingertips. So, when she grabbed her husband's beard, she ended up putting ten holes in his chin with her fingernails.

Everything calmed back down for the night.

The next morning, Rose watched her mom sit down and write some stuff on a piece of paper, and she asked the lady that lived upstairs, (which just so happened to be her so-called best friend's mother), if she would take the paper the next day and get it notarized. Immediately following that, her mom walked into the kitchen, opened the knife drawer, and got a knife out. Rose screamed, "Oh my god, she's gonna try to kill herself," and ran out the door and down the alley and begged her dad to come help stop her mom. Scared and sad, she ran back down the alley towards her mother's place.

As she re-entered the house, her oldest brother said, "She wasn't trying to kill herself, she was just cutting potatoes." As soon as he said that, their mother turned the knife to her stomach and tried pushing it in. "Mom, no stop," Rose screamed as the neighbor and her oldest brother wrestled her mother to the ground to get the knife from her.

When her mother got up off the floor, she grabbed a ceramic flowerpot and hit herself over the head, breaking the flowerpot. Everyone finally got her to sit down, and then she started burning herself with her lit cigarette. By now, Rose had called everyone that she could to try to get someone over there to help stop her mom from hurting herself. Finally, as her mom grabbed a full glass soda bottle and tried to hit herself in the head with it, a hand swooped in and snatched the bottle from her. It was Rose's cousin. Thank God, cause that meant that her aunt and uncle were there. Rose's uncle was a very large and strong man, and it took everything he had to keep her mom in the chair until the police and ambulance arrived. Rose then watched them handcuff her mother and put her on a gurney in the back of the ambulance. She was taken to the psych ward at St. Lukes.

Barb came to pick Rose up after that and was very angry that Rose had to deal with all that on her first-weekend visit. Her mother remained in the hospital for about a week and a half. When her mother got home. She seemed to be handling things a little better. She was talking about finding a new man. And she had just learned that her oldest son and his girlfriend were expecting. She was elated, as this would be her first grandchild.

However, around the time her mother got out of the hospital, the departure date for Rose to go to Colorado was almost there. Rose started having this dream that when she was in Colorado, something had happened to her mom. Well, the dream didn't happen just once, but like three or four nights in a row. Rose then tells Barb, "Barb, I can't go to Colorado. Something's gonna happen to my mom if I go." Barb tried to reassure her, "Rose, you've waited on this for a long time. Why don't you just go and enjoy yourself?" "Barb, seriously, I can't go. I keep having this dream that something happens to my mom when I'm gone." "Rose, you're going. You've been worrying about adult issues for way too long. You need to go be a kid for once and enjoy yourself," Barb replied. Rose lost the argument. So, she went and visited her mom, who was so happy that she was going to be a grandma. She promised to take lots of pictures to share with her mom when she returned. She kissed and hugged her mother and told her that she loved her.

Rose left for Colorado the following day. It took two days to get to Colorado, as they had stopped at a church in

Nebraska the first night. The morning after they got to Colorado, they started the long trek up the mountain. All the kids were exhausted when they reached the top and were ready to set up camp, eat some food, and relax.

Rose did enjoy herself and took at least four rolls of pictures, and couldn't wait to get back to Iowa to show her mom the pictures of how beautiful it was there. The trip back to Iowa took two days, also with a layover in Nebraska.

As the vans full of children pulled back up to the Children's home, Rose was scanning the parking lot looking for Barb's car. "Huh, she must be running late," Rose thought to herself. Once Rose gathered her belongings, one of the staff members approached her with a note from Barb. The note read, "Hey sweetie, I hope you had an amazing time. I had some errands to run, so they are gonna take you to your grandmother's house, and I will pick you up when I finish. Love, Barb." Rose is already sensing that something isn't right.

The staff member pulled up in her grandmother's driveway, and Rose saw two of her aunts, who didn't get along, looking out her grandma's living room door. "Why are they both here together? They don't even like each other," Rose thought to herself. "And why is Grandma's front door open?

It's never been open because nobody is allowed to use the front door." As all these thoughts raced through her mind, Rose walked up the stairs that go around to her grandma's side door. Her Grandmother opened the front door and said, "Come here, honey."

She knew it. It really was just as she had thought. It was her mom, it had to be, or they wouldn't all be there. As she walked into the living room, she looked at her favorite Aunt, and asked, "Where's mom?" "Rose, put your things down," her aunt replied. Rose busted into tears, and then went into a seizure. Come to find out, her mother had passed the previous morning, and they waited till she got back to tell her for fear of her having a seizure, as she just had. She died on 8-18-1988 at ten minutes till two in the morning. She died of an abdominal aortic aneurysm caused by a heart attack.

As they finally got Rose seated and she started to calm down, her father came through the side door off of her grandma's kitchen. Rose busted into tears again and ran to her father, as he held her for a moment, and then said, "I'm sorry sissy, I wanted to tell you. I have to go for now, but I'll see you tomorrow, ok?" She nodded and went back to sit at her grandma's table. Next, her uncle and Jayson come in through the side door. She ran to her brother. They both stood there hugging and sobbing for what seemed like an eternity, before taking a seat back at the table. Jayson and their uncle were talking about a car/train accident that they had just seen. Rose stayed at her grandma's till about nine that night, when Barb came to pick her up. Barb held Rose and just kept saying, "I'm so sorry sweetie, I didn't know." How could she have known? She had only done what she thought was the right thing to do.

As Rose and Barb left her grandmother's that night, Rose begged Barb to take her to her best friend's house. Her best friend was actually the daughter of her dad's current woman.

When they arrived there, Rose asked where she was and was told that she was at Mercy Hospital because the car/train accident that her uncle and Jayson spoke of was actually one of their friends, and they didn't think he was going to make it. Let's say he was in the hospital for over a year and then lived with handicaps as a result. However, he did make it through.

The week of her mother's death, Barb was extremely concerned about Rose's depression and was scared that Rose may try to harm herself or, even worse, try to commit suicide. So, Barb kept

Rose extremely close to her and even allowed her to lay in her bed with her. In fact, for the first couple of nights, Barb would stroke her hair as she cried herself to sleep. Barb almost felt guilt and responsibility since she had made Rose go to Colorado. However, Rose never blamed her or felt that Barb's decision wasn't in Rose's best interest.

The following morning, Rose rejoined Jayson and other family members back at her grandmother's, as they were to go to the funeral home that day for the viewing. As Rose entered the room where her mother laid in the casket, she became extremely dizzy. She was afraid to even look towards the casket. Sobbing uncontrollably and feeling like the whole world was spinning, she took a seat in a chair. Eventually, she slowed down her breathing, and the tears slowed a little; she got up and walked up to the casket. It looked like her mom was lying there, but with the makeup and stuff on her, it kind of didn't look like her mom.

As she stood there, she wanted to touch her mother, just to put her hand on her mother's hand. She tried once and just couldn't make herself do it. One of her cousins, who was standing next to her, asked, "Do you want to touch her?" "C'mon, I'll help you," they said. "Put your hand on top of mine." So, she did. Her cousin then put his hand on top of her mother's hand and then slowly slid his hand out from in between. She held it there for only a couple of seconds till she had had enough for then. She quickly disappeared outside for a cigarette. She spent as little time as possible in the room with the casket that day. It was just too much for her, and to be honest, it kind of creeped her out.

Two days later would be the day of the funeral. Rose was having a lot of anxiety about not having anything to wear to her mother's funeral. All she knew was what she had seen on TV: when someone died, everyone wore black. Barb told Rose that she was welcome to pick something out of her closet to wear. Rose was still stressed, because she couldn't find a black outfit in Barb's clothes. It was then that Barb explained that people did use to only wear black during a funeral, but that in more current times, people wore lots of different things during funerals. Rose settled on a red Barb's dress that she had liked since the first time Barb allowed her to look in her closet for something to wear. In fact, it was part of the clothes that Barb had told her were off limits the first day she moved in, but this was an important day, and Barb wanted to make the clothes selection an easy process since there wasn't anything easy about the remainder of her week. Barb found Rose some jewelry to wear with the dress.

As family and friends gathered at the funeral home, Rose happened to look over to the door just as her Aunt LuAnn walked in. "Oh my god, It's Aunt LuAnn," she thought to herself. "How does she know?" None of that mattered as her Aunt

LuAnn walked straight to Rose and wrapped her arms around her. She hugged Rose so close and tight that it was as if the broken pieces that Rose's week caused, were being squeezed back together. In fact, her Aunt Lu Ann hugged her so hard, one of Rose's earrings came out.

Eventually, everyone took their seats, and the services began. Rose's grandmother's best friend then stands to sing Amazing Grace. The whole place was in tears. She could not have sung it any more beautifully. Soon, the services wrapped up, and the eight pallbearers walked out with the casket and loaded it into the hearse. All but one of the pallbearers were either cousins or uncles to the children (of which one of them was the cousin that had hurt and traumatized her just a couple of years ago). However, that would be the last time that she had to see him, because shortly after her mother's funeral, she heard that he was in prison for murder. And so, the procession began to Oak Hill Cemetery, where they would lay her to rest. The kids joined their mother's five sisters and grandmother in the little row of seats while the minister gave his little eulogy. Everyone started to load back into their cars. Many of them would meet back up at their grandmother's house. However, the three children and a couple of their cousins stayed behind. They wanted to smoke some weed before they went back to their grandma's house. All three kids watched their mother's casket be lowered into the ground.

As they arrived back at their grandmother's house, Rose didn't feel much like socializing, and she definitely couldn't fathom the idea of eating anything at that time. She went into her grandma's den, where it was much quieter. She just sat in there crying, when Aunt LuAnn joined her. Aunt LuAnn sat down on the couch and said to Rose, "Come here, baby girl." She held Rose in her arms and stroked her hair, till she cried herself to sleep. Once she knew Rose would be okay, she left and started her two-hour journey back home to Ft. Madison, Iowa.

Rose had started 8th grade around the time of her mother's death. She continued to live with Barb, and eventually started visits with her father.

The first time she went to visit her father was very emotionally difficult for Rose, as he, his woman, and many of her family were now residing in her mother's home. In fact, her dad's girlfriend and some of her sisters were wearing her mother's clothes. Her father and this woman were sleeping in her mother's bed.

As the remainder of 1988 wrapped up, Rose just continued school at Prairie, and continued visiting with her father. Barb and she had become really close after the death of her mother. There were some other foster kids that had come and gone, as well as some that currently resided at Barb's. As a matter of fact, Barb had adopted one of her foster daughters. As the winter months were upon them, so was Rose's birthday.

Chapter 14
Age 15

Rose was now 15 years old and most of the way through her 8th grade year. She hated attending Prairie. She hated listening to classmates ' torment every day. She couldn't wait for the school year to end. As the end of the school year neared, Barb had heard that they were gonna send Rose back home to live with her father.

Neither Barb, nor Rose was sure how they felt about that. Barb was concerned for Rose's well-being, and Rose just didn't want to live with him. He was the main reason that she had left her home, to begin with. She feared him in more ways than one.

Around this time, her father and her mom's friend married. Rose refused to be part of it or to attend, as did her oldest step sister.

Well, that didn't stop their plans. As the 8th grade year ended, the day also came that Rose's father was coming to pick her up. By the time he pulled into the driveway, her foster sisters had helped her carry her belongings outside the front door. It's crazy how much stuff she was returning back home with, just a year and a half later after arriving at Barb's with just the clothes on her back. After her belongings were loaded, she said goodbye to her foster sisters, which made her kind of emotional. Then came time for her to say goodbye to Barb. Rose had grown to love this woman who opened her home, but more importantly, her heart to Rose. She was the only adult who encouraged Rose and spoke to her with any inspiration. They stood there for the better part of a half hour, hugging and crying. Rose was gonna truly miss Barb. However, Barb reassured her that she would always be there for her.

Once back at her father's, Rose's file with DHS was closed. Rose spent a lot of time in the basement in her mom's old house. In fact, she had started dating this 23-year-old who had a motorcycle. This, truthfully, would be the first male that Rose would say that she was actually in love with.

Sometimes, he would stay with her, and sometimes, she would stay at his house. As a matter of fact, he broke his ankle one night as he slipped going down the basement stairs.

One day, as Rose got off his bike as he dropped her off at home, she bumped the inside of her calf on his exhaust pipe. It hurt really bad, cause it was a pretty serious burn. Rose didn't know the proper way to care for a burn. She kept it clean in the way that she cleaned it when she bathed. About a week and a half later, she was having pains all the way up to her groin area. So, she decided to go to the hospital. The ER staff told her she was lucky that she had come in when she did, because gangrene was about to set in, and she could have lost her leg. They had to remove all the dry dead skin. Thankfully, they administered some pain meds before they began the skin removal.

Rose followed all of the doctor's orders completely until her leg healed.

The following month, everyone would be moving out of her mother's home. As a matter of fact, they were moving to a house in Belle Plaine, Iowa. As they were loading the Uhaul, Rose's oldest brother showed up. He asked Rose, "Do you want to smoke some bud?" "Sure," she replied. So, they went down to the basement and put some weed in a pipe, and began smoking it. All of a sudden, he said to Rose, "Let me lick your pussy." Rose replied, "No, obviously you haven't figured out yet that brothers and sisters don't do those kinds of things. If you can't get it from your girlfriend, then there are plenty of females on the streets giving theirs away." "Let me just touch it then," he said to her. "No," she said again. "Can I at least see it?" he asked. This time, she didn't even respond, she simply went back upstairs and went back to work on loading the truck. He came upstairs after a couple of minutes, and left out of the door.

So, later that night, once everything was loaded, they drove to the house in Belle Plaine. It only took a month until the seven adults in the house couldn't get it together for the nine children in the house. So, when they didn't pay the rent that month, they were evicted. They really had nowhere to go, so most of their belongings went into a storage unit, and all 16 members of the household were now in tents and cars at a campground. The following day, Rose had heard one of the adults say that they had contacted a local news station, and they were going to come the following day to do a news story about them. I guess the adult's thought process was that some nice soul would help them all get housing, which was insane. They would still have housing if the adults would have just paid the bills.

Rose decided she'd had enough. She didn't have a phone number for Jayson, but she was able to find his girlfriend's number in the phone book.

Later that evening, she came to the campground and picked up Rose and two of her step-siblings. The three of them ran away. They definitely didn't want to be interviewed by the news station, much less have their faces on the news.

Jayson's girlfriend had driven three hours to pick them up, and now the four of them were making the three-hour trip back. She explained that Jayson wasn't home, but she expected him back anytime. She had a key to Jayson's house, so she let them in and said she would check back the following day. They made something to eat and just relaxed and watched TV.

The following day, they took Jayson's cans and bottles back to the store so that they could get cigarettes. They didn't hear from his girlfriend until the following day, when she brought some alcoholic beverages to share with them. However, after she had consumed a couple of drinks, she decided that she was angry at Jayson for not being home yet, so she ended up punching a couple of holes in his bedroom walls. After she left and it was just the three of them again, Rose and her step-sister were laying on Jayson's waterbed, when all of a sudden, her step-brother came running into the room and jumped on the bed in between the two girls, and the front side rail of the bed gave way, causing half of the waterbed mattress to roll onto the floor. Rose wondered how she would explain that situation to her brother.

Jayson didn't show up until about a week and a half after the three had arrived there. He came in the middle of the night and told his sister to pack up his stuff, and he would be back in the middle of the night the following day. She explained what had happened to the bedroom wall, as well as the waterbed, and he just laughed. Then he asked her, "Sissy, have you been feeding my turtle?" "What was I supposed to feed it?" she asked in return.

The turtle was dead. He asked if she had taken his clothes out of the washer. She hadn't even thought to look in the washer for any reason, so his clothes in there were ruined due to mildew. He again said to pack his things, and that he would see her the next day. He also said if the girlfriend asked, to tell her that they still hadn't heard from him.

He returned the next night in the middle of the night, as promised. It was him and his uncle in a pickup truck. Rose asked how they were all gonna ride. Well, let's just say the three of them took turns riding in the front, while the other two rode laying down in the back on top of Jayson's belongings, while half freezing under a couple blankets. It was not a pleasant two-hour ride for any of them.

They pulled into Cedar Rapids, and Jayson told his sister that he was dropping the three of them off at their oldest brother's house and that he was going to go with his uncle to take his stuff to Lamont, Iowa, to store at Jayson's father's house.

The next morning, her stepbrother and sister went back home to their mother. Jayson was back at her oldest brother's by the afternoon.

Rose and Jayson stayed there for a couple of months through the winter.

Chapter 15
Age 16-17

As January brought in a new year, Rose was now 16 years old. Wherever Jayson was, Rose was with him. They did a lot of hanging out that year with friends, smoking weed, and just kind of having fun. Around her nephew's 1st birthday, they learned that their oldest brother's girlfriend was pregnant with their second child. Rose worked really hard over a three-week period. She cleaned her oldest brother's place from top to bottom to getit clean, sanitary, and ready to bring home a new baby.

The year went by fairly quickly. Rose andJayson worked jobs a little here and there for money. And sometimes, when they weren't working, they would go to stores like K-Mart, Target, Jack's, or Walmart, and someone would go in and steal something, and the other person would go back in and return. It was a quick way to get a little money for gas, cigarettes, food, etc. If we're being honest, these were the things they had done their whole lives, because that's what their parents taught them to do at a young age.

It was early December that year, when Rose and Jayson were walking to the gas station from their brother's house. They decided to take a different route than what they normally took. While taking this route, as they walked by this one house, there were two females in an upstairs window, and they were whistling and making comments to Jayson. Well after they were finished getting cigarettes and soda at the store, they took their normal route back to their brother's house.

Jayson told his oldest brother and his girlfriend about the two females yelling out the window, and explained which house it was. Well, his brother's girlfriend said, "I know who lives there. Do you want to meet them?" "Hell yeah," Jayson replied. So, she walked with the two of them back down to the house they had passed. They knocked on the door and everyone was introduced. Funny enough the two females that were yelling out the window thought that Rose was his girlfriend and that Rose was coming back to fight them for yelling at her man. Nope, that's her brother, and she didn't care that they were hollering at him. In fact, Rose and Jayson stayed and partied with the two girls that night. Next thing you knew, Jayson was dating the girl that actually lived there, and Rose and her had become quick friends. When they met, this friend had a 4-month-old daughter with whom Rose quickly fell in love. This female, Jayson, and Rose were inseparable for the remainder of the year.

One day, as Rose and her friend were talking, Rose said to her, "Hey, I want you to write this down somewhere or something. When I die, there are three songs that I want to be played at my service. The first one is Stairway to Heaven by Led Zepplin, then Knocking on Heaven's Door by Guns N Roses, and lastly, Momma I'm Coming Home by Ozzy Osbourne."

She looked at Rose, shocked, and said, "That's so crazy." "What's crazy?" Rose asked her. She said, "I swear to God, two days ago, Jayson sat here and told me the exact same thing. And he listed the same three songs in the exact same order." That was crazy; that was a discussion that Jayson and

Rose had never had. But yet they somehow had both said the same thing to her. Perhaps you could say that over the years, Jayson and Rose had gotten so close that it's almost like they had a bit of telepathy between them.

Before you knew it, January rang in a new year, and Rose was now 17. It was about a third of the way through the year when Rose got caught stealing at Walmart and was taken downtown to the police station. She was sitting in this little interrogation-type room, scared to death, when the door opened, and in walked Jayson. As Jayson sat next to her and the door shut, he said to his sister, "Don't even trip sissy. When we get out of here, we're gonna get high. Look what I picked up on the way here," he said as he pulled a nice sized bag out of his pocket. "Oh my god, put that away. Are you serious? You're gonna get me in so much more trouble. I'm serious, Jayson put it away," Rose said. They ended up releasing Rose to Jayson, as he was her closest next of kin and was over 18.

As the two of them got in Jayson's car out front of the police station, Jayson lit one joint and started passing it around. And then he lit a second and third one, all while still in front of the police station. "Jayson, honestly, can we please just go?" she asked in an irritated tone. Jayson just laughed, "Oh sissy, I thought you said you wanted to get high." The two of them had even enjoyed tripping on acid from time to time. They were really just two teens completely unsupervised by adults. Given that, Rose always had to be the most responsible one, because Jayson always took partying to the extreme.

When Rose went to court for the theft charge, she was ordered to return to Barb's house until she was 18. One day, Jayson and Rose's best friend showed up at Barb's and asked if Rose could go to the park with them for a little while. Rose's friend had to show Barb her license and proof of insurance, and she had to promise that she would bring her back. Once they were in the car pulling away from Barb's, Jayson said to Rose, "Guess what I'm doing tonight?" "What?" Rose asked. "I'm eating acid," he replied. "Well, if you're eating acid, then I'm eating acid," she said to him. "Sissy, you can't do that. I just promised Barb that I'll bring you back," he responded. She again said, "If you're eating acid, then I'm eating acid." Jayson shrugged his shoulders at the point and said, "Okay, I guess we're eating acid then."

That night, there were about seven or eight teens on the high side of the roller dam tripping on acid, when all of a sudden, the police helicopter lowers down where he is right in front of them and just hovered there for a few minutes before flying away. Rose was hiding on the back floor of her brother's, freaking out, screaming at Jayson, "Don't let them take me to jail, Jay, please don't let them take me." "Jayson was trying to calm and reassure his sister while trying to remain calm himself. That had to be the only bad trip that Rose had ever had. As a matter of fact, she woke the next morning with the word acid tattooed on her arm. Jayson didn't like that some boy had tattooed his initials on Rose's arm, so he turned them into the word acid. When she asked him, he said, "You told me I could turn it into something else, so I did." They sure were a force to reckon with sometimes, but they had a lot of fun that year.

Rose still lived at her oldest brother's house, but wasn't there a lot as she was at her new friend's house. However, one night, as Rose was sleeping on a fold-up bed in a room in the front of her oldest brother's house, she woke with a startle because she could sense that someone was near her. As she jumped, she opened her eyes. She didn't see anyone, until she looked over her shoulder. There was a reason she sensed someone near her. It was her oldest brother who was kneeling beside her bed. In one quick motion, she was now sitting up facing him. She was trembling, with tears in her eyes. She said, "I swear to god, you better get the fuck away from me. I swear, your whole fucking house is about to be awake, and I promise I'm leaving here in handcuffs, and you'll either be going to the hospital or the morgue."

It was at that very moment that she felt as though she could very well take her oldest brother's life. This was indeed the first time that she felt homicidal, and it absolutely horrified her. Her brother quickly retreated to the living room couch, where he sat watching porn and playing with himself. Rose lay in the dark after that with tears in her eyes, saddened that her brother was still trying to have sex with her. She had wished that one day he would grow up and stop the sexual acts. The next morning, before the members of the house woke up, Rose packed up her belongings.

The homicidal feeling that she had that night scared her enough to know that she had to leave there before the thoughts became her reality.

She had no idea where she would go, but she knew for certain that she couldn't stay there any longer.

Where did she go when she left that day? Is she okay? Did she survive the demons of her childhood? Were any of the people who did all those horrible things to her made to be held accountable for their actions? What about Jayson? Was he able to go on and live a normal life? Did either of them have a family? If so, are their children okay, or were they raised the way that Rose and Jayson were raised?

What about the oldest brother? What happened to him? Did he ever get help and break the cycle of the sexual predator behavior that he had been engaging in since such a young age? Was Rose able to forgive any of the people who had hurt her?

Chapter 16

I am happy to report that both Rose and Jayson did survive. You see, the reason I know their story so well is because that was my story. Hi, I'm Rose. Now, I'd like to reflect on some of the experiences I've lived through and discuss what life has been like as adults. As well as update you on what Rose and Jayson have been doing in their lives, after surviving the hell that they knew as their childhood. I am currently 48 and we are officially 4 days away from celebrating Jayson's 50th birthday.

When I left my oldest brother's house all those years ago, I, in fact, moved in with the friend that Jayson and I met by chance the day we walked to the store. I helped a lot with her daughter's care and was working, so I was also able to contribute to the bills. This person was now my best friend.

She was like the sister that I never had. In 1992, Jayson and his girlfriend at the time, welcomed a beautiful baby girl into the world. She was born on September 3rd. Unfortunately, a few months after his daughter was born, Jayson was arrested on charges of burglary. Imagine that, arrested for the same thing that he was programmed and made to do his entire childhood, "Stealing." He received a five-year sentence and was sent to Mt. Pleasant penitentiary. He in total spent 38 months incarcerated. He had missed out on all of his daughter's firsts. In fact, she barely knew who he was when he was released.

In 1993, while Jayson was in prison, I met who would end up being the father of my children at my job at Burger King.

The manager had just offered him a position, and when trying to figure out a schedule for him, the manager asked when was the earliest time that he could be there each day. He told the manager that he was currently a resident at the halfway house, and would need to ride public transportation to and from work. Well let's just say the manager called me over, since I too used public transportation to ask what time my bus arrived at that location each morning. A couple of days later, he started working with me, and we quickly became familiar with each other while riding the bus to get home each day.

He had just gotten out of prison after being locked up for forgery at the age of 18, which would have been five years prior. I think more than anything I was drawn to him, because of his story. You see, he had been given up for adoption from his birth mother when he was three. He was adopted by a couple who had two children of their own. Well at the age of 7, he developed juvenile diabetes. This is not something the adopted parents had anticipated and the medical bills started piling up. By the time he was 10, his adoptive parents had decided that the medical bills and such were just too much to handle, so one day they dropped him off at Cromwell, in Independence, Iowa. Which yes this is the same place where Jayson had spent some time during his childhood. They told him that they would return to get him in a week but never returned.

A short time later, he met a couple who only had one biological child of their own. They had a very young daughter, and they were looking for an older brother for her. They then welcomed him to their family. This couple would be the ones that my children grew up knowing and loving as their grandparents.

When I met my children's father, I lived in a two-bedroom apartment. I had my brother's daughter and her mother who were staying with me at the time, kind of as a favor for Jayson. He asked me to look after his daughter since he was locked up and couldn't be there. That lasted until her boyfriend beat her up one day, and then three days later he was back at my house when I got home from work one day. He had a pistol that he was messing around with. Now, myself being a small-town girl, I had never seen a pistol before. I said, "I don't think I could shoot anyone, unless of course I had children and someone hurt one of them." At that time, he popped the clip back in the bottom, put the tip of the gun against my temple, and said, "Piss me off Bitch, and I'll shoot you." Later that day, when the two of them left, I grabbed everything I needed out of that apartment, called my father, and the children's father and I went to Grinnell, Iowa to an apartment building where my father lived. We only slept on his floor for about 2 days before we moved upstairs to an efficiency apartment.

While I lived in the same building as my father, there was something on my mind that made it heavy. So, one day I said to my father, "I need to ask you something. I already know the truth and answer to this question, but I want to hear it from you." I then said to him the following, "That night, you know that you and I were home alone? You know the night you asked me that question, you know when you asked me if I wanted to fool around?" "Yes," he simply replied. "Okay, well then here is my question. When you caught up to me that day, you still had on the same clothes, and your hair was still dry, which means you never got in the tub.

What I really want to know is, if you closed that door to take a bath, why did you come out of the bathroom if you weren't finished with your bath?"

"Umm… I don't know," he replied. So I said to him again, "When you closed the bathroom door that day, you were gonna take a bath, correct?" "Yes," he answered again. "Then why didn't you get in the bathtub?" I asked him again. Again, he replied, "I don't know." I then asked the same questions again, and again. I then asked him, "Had I not of left that day, you had came out of the bathroom to do whatever you wanted to do to me, correct?" "If I didn't leave that day, you would have raped me," I said. "That's why you came out of the bathroom without getting in the tub, isn't it?" I asked him again. The first couple of times, he denied it. So I said to him, "I'm not gonna let this go until you give me a real answer." He then replied, Okay, fine, you're right, okay? There I answered, are you happy now?" I said, "I already knew the answer, I've replayed that night over and over in my mind. I just wanted you to admit to it."

Crazy, had I not taken off that day and created that little period of time, my father would have raped me. That is a hard reality to live with. I would never trust him again, the way I once did. In that one single night, he robbed me of my Daddy. He went from being the man I felt the safest around to being the man that I feared the most.

I have to admit that while living at this residence, Jayson and I ran up over a thousand-dollar phone bill talking on the phone. This is also where my children's father proposed to me.

Our oldest brother had 3 children with the girlfriend that he was with when our mother was still alive. In 1994, he and his new girlfriend brought his fourth child into the world, and then his 5th child the following year in 1995.

It was also in 1995, on October 27th, that I married my children's father. Jayson was still incarcerated at the time, but it wasn't long after that Jayson discharged his sentence and was released from prison. In the over three years that Jayson was locked up, he and I wrote tons of letters back and forth, in fact, I still have the letters from my brother. I only visited him two times, because it was extremely hard for me emotionally. After all, I couldn't even hug him when I went to see him. As well as the fact that it ripped my heart when we had to say our goodbyes again. I hated that I couldn't take him home with me, and I hated to see him tear up as our visit ended. It was a story we knew all too well from all the time that he was institutionalized during our childhood. The day did finally arrive that I received my final letter from him which was only written on about a third of a sheet of paper. Also enclosed was a poem that he had written for his daughter. The letter simply read.

Dear Sissy, I'll be home on Friday. I wrote this poem for my daughter. Please put it up and keep it safe, because I want to give it to her someday when she's a little older. I love you and I'll see you in a couple of days. Love Jayson. I was so elated that my brother was finally coming home, that I think I was teary-eyed for the rest of the week.

Everyone I encountered that week, I just had to tell them, "My brother will be home on this date." The day that he was released from prison, I had a bouquet of balloons, I ordered pizza, and had a cake especially made for him, that read, "Welcome home." The funny thing was, when he walked in, I was instantly in tears, elated that he was finally free of paper.

Well, let's just say, he gave me a hug and said, "I'm glad I'm home Sissy." Then he told me that he had to run somewhere real quick, well let's just say I didn't see my brother again for about a week and a half. You see, earlier that year, my brothers, as well as myself had received a check for $2,215. That was inheritance money from our grandmother passing away. Because her will was as such: if she passed before any of her daughters, the money would be split evenly between the six girls. However, if any of her daughters passed before she did, that daughter's money would be divided between that daughter's children. So since Jayson was incarcerated, that money was released to him the day he got out of prison. The partying had begun. The day he got out, he ate 15 hits of acid. And that was just the very beginning of the celebration. Jayson and the mother of his child didn't get back together, in fact, she had more children, 4 in total. It was around this time that Jayson got wrapped up in the meth scene. And he liked the needle high the best. He literally would be up for a week or better at a time. He ran dope from one side of Iowa to the other.

One day, as we were at Jayson's uncle's house, Jayson and my best friend said that they were going to run to a town somewhere not too far away.

I agreed to watch her daughter. They didn't return for like three days. When they did come back they told everyone how they had just about both just almost lost their lives. She had been asleep in the passenger seat, and let's just say Jayson had been up for over a week. All of a sudden, Jayson sat up, as he had just fallen out, slumped over to the passenger side. When he sat back up and looked out his side window, they were flying sideways down the highway, and when he looked at the dash, the speedometer read 80 mph. By the grace of God, somehow he managed to get the car stopped on the right side of the road facing the right direction. Thankfully, they were safe. Had I lost my brother and friend that day, that would have ruined me.

It was around the end of 1996 that Jayson did such a large amount of dope that he was freaking out swinging hammers and such around thinking that people were after him.

It was also around this time that he got off the dope for a while and was now dating our oldest brother's first baby momma. He had agreed that he was going to help raise his brother's children since he really wasn't an active participant. As a matter of fact, my husband and I lived there with them at the time, because I would watch my niece and nephew while their mother went to school. By this time, I really wanted a baby of my own. My husband and I had been together for almost four years, and had never used contraception, but still, I had never become pregnant. It was around the time of my twenty-third birthday that I called The University of Iowa Hospital to schedule a fertility test.

Much to my surprise, I never made it to that appointment. You see, when February rolled around, I missed my menstrual cycle. I had always been on a schedule my entire life that my period came religiously on almost the exact same date every month. When it was a week past when my period should have started, I went and had a pregnancy test done, that confirmed that I was indeed pregnant. I honestly don't think that I could have been any more elated and excited than I was the minute they said the test was positive. My husband and I decided, at this time, that we needed to get our own place so that we could start preparing for the arrival of our first child. So we rented a two-bedroom apartment.

By the time we got moved into our place, the mother of Jayson's daughter had gotten into some legal issues, so Jayson's daughter along with her siblings had been put in protective custody by the Department of Human Services. I offered the other bedroom to Jayson at that time, so that he would have a safe stable place to have visits with his daughter with the hopes that maybe eventually he would get custody of her. It wasn't long until Jayson's visits with his daughter were taken away. They weren't taken away due to any abuse or neglect, but because he wasn't doing everything they required for him to do. He was supposed to get a full-time job, go to NA classes, parenting classes, and much more. I was fairly upset with my brother, when he said to me, "Sissy, it's not humanly possible for me to do everything that they require me to do." I was mad at him for saying that, "What do you mean not possible," I thought to myself. Little did either of us know, that within about six months of this day, Jayson was diagnosed with schizophrenia. In fairness, for his situation, being undiagnosed, and not being treated for his condition, it truly wasn't possible for him to do everything they required.

Soon after they stopped Jayson's visits, he went back to live with the mother of our oldest brother's children. And my husband and I moved into the basement of my father's house, because I was so sick during my pregnancy that I couldn't work, therefore, we couldn't afford the apartment.

Chapter 17

It was during the summer of my first pregnancy that our oldest brother had been living in an apartment with his girlfriend at the time.

Jayson was still dating the mother of our niece and nephews. Well, all of a sudden one day, it was obvious that our brother had moved out of his apartment without alerting anyone that he was going anywhere. It's like he just disappeared into thin air.

It was around this time that Jayson went upstairs to the house he shared with our niece and nephews and their mother. He went up because the children were extremely quiet. As he entered one of the kids' bedrooms, he saw our niece performing oral sex on her brother, who was a year younger than her. Instantly Jayson spanked both children and separated them, then went downstairs to talk with their mother and also to calm down.

After a short time, they talked to both children to find out where they had learned that behavior.

First, they talked to the niece. When they asked her who taught her that, she responded with, "I like to have sex with my dad and ******," which was the name of her dad's girlfriend. They immediately got the children's doctor and such involved.

Fortunately, he hadn't penetrated his daughter.

But unfortunately, there were no charges filed against either one of them, as they said it would be their word against our niece's word. How disgusting is that? So, basically, this sexually twisted mother fucker that had molested me for all those years, had now been engaging in oral sex acts with my niece, his own daughter? And to make it worse, his girlfriend was involved also.

And absolutely nothing could be done about it.

That's why the coward left unexpectedly, without alerting anyone. All I hoped at that point was that wherever he went, he would stay there, because if Jayson ever saw him after that moment in the children's bedroom, he would and still will kill him. I know that I didn't and still don't want him around my children, especially my daughter, because I too would kill him.

Chapter 18

My due date for my daughter was Oct. 30th.

Surprisingly enough, even though rarely do women go into labor on their actual due date, I did. I woke up around 5 am on the morning of October 30th, because my back was really hurting. As I used the restroom, I quickly realized that I had lost my mucus plug. The pain in my lower back would come and go. It felt almost like someone would squeeze my lower back, for a minute or so, and then release, then squeeze again, then release. I was definitely having contractions, just in my back instead of my lower abdomen. Around 7 am, I was scared and anxious with this being my first child, so I went to the hospital to get checked out. While in the exam room, I threw up all over the floor, after a fairly powerful contraction.

When they examined me, they said that I was only dilated 2 centimeters. So they had me walk the halls of the hospital for an hour to see if that would help progress labor. Unfortunately, when they checked me after that hour, they said that I was still only dilated to 2. They sent me home and told me that if the contractions get stronger and closer together, to come back to the hospital. Let's just say, all day long I had these contractions in my back every 3 to 5 minutes. We went to a Halloween party at a company that evening. After I had eaten a hot dog and a small bag of chips, the contractions got so strong that I threw up again.

I decided to return to the hospital to see if anything had changed. This time when they checked me, I was 3 centimeters. Again, they had me walk the halls for an hour.

When they checked me that time, I had finally reached 4 centimeters. So, they told me that they were going to admit me. Finally, 18 hours after the contractions had started. They said that they were going to let me take a whirlpool bath, and then they were going to inject me with some morphine to take the edge off of the contractions, so that I could rest for a while. The morphine knocked me out for about 4 hours or so.

All of a sudden, I woke up with what seemed at the time, an extreme urgency to use the restroom. As soon as I sat down on the toilet, I knew that I didn't have to use the restroom. What I was feeling was pressure from the baby. I was now 8.5 centimeters dilated. They broke my water, and started Pitocin, which made the dilation decrease a little. When I finally reached 9 centimeters, they cut me to allow a little more room for her to come out. When I reached 9.5 they told me that I could start pushing with contractions. I never did dilate to a full 10 centimeters, instead, they stretched the rest of the cervix around her head.

After an hour of pushing, my baby girl had finally made her arrival. But wait a minute, why didn't I hear her crying? As I waited for her to cry, I heard the doctor say, "Scissors, stat." I just laid there listening. I couldn't see, because they had sheets draped over my legs. As soon as the doctor was handed the scissors, you could hear her umbilical cord unravel. Her cord was wrapped around her neck a couple of times. Finally, after what seemed like an eternity, I heard her cry. I burst into tears. My baby is finally here, and she's crying, that means she's ok. When they laid my baby girl into my arms for the first time, and I looked down at her precious little face, it was right at that very moment that I actually felt what love was.

She had made her arrival into the world on 10-31-1997 at 10:28 am, weighing in at 7lbs 3oz, and she was twenty inches long. My little Halloween baby. She was absolutely perfect. I never did let the nurses take her to the nursery. I had waited all these years for this moment, and I wasn't letting my princess, Angelica out of my sight.

Everything about her was perfect, from the head full of blonde hair, which I could put the top into a ponytail the day she was born. To her beautiful little blue eyes, her tiny little nose, her cute little pouty lips, her cute little fingers that she would hold onto my finger with, and all the way down to her tiny little toes. I couldn't get enough of her. And every time I looked at her, there would be tears in my eyes, I just couldn't believe that this one was finally mine to take home and love. I promised that she would never live the horror of sexual abuse, or beatings, or having to steal to help support the house, as I had at such a young age.

Two days later, she and I both received medical clearance and we were able to go home. We were still in the basement at my father's house. I showed her off to everyone I knew, but I only let people hold her for maybe a total of five minutes before I wanted her back in my arms.

Shortly after we brought our beautiful daughter home, my oldest step-sister and her family moved out into their own home, so my husband, daughter, and I transferred out of the basement and into a bedroom on the upstairs level of the house. Before long the house was full of people, as all of my stepmother's other five children, their partners, children, and even friends had moved in. My stepmom's one sister, her two daughters, and her new fiancé moved in. In total, there were now about 25 people in a 5-bedroom house. I'm not sure who brought them, but the house was now infested with cockroaches, and nobody on the main level of the house ever wanted to clean, which didn't help the bug situation.

When my daughter was a year and a half old, one of my stepsisters thought that she might be pregnant, and was scared about going to get a pregnancy test. I told her, "Girl it's not a big deal, you literally just pee in a cup and they come in a couple minutes later and tell you the results." "C'mon, I'll go pee in a cup too, just to make it more comfortable for you," I said to her. Well long story short, it turned out that her test was negative. Mine, on the other hand, ended up being positive. I was only going to help her relax, and here I was the one coming back to the house with a positive test.

Wow, I guess we will be adding to our family in about 8 more months. I really wanted for us to get our own place now, however, it seemed every month, I had to keep putting in extra money for bills, because others who lived there wouldn't pay their share. So, it was decided that in January as soon as we filed our taxes, we would move.

One day in November, as some of us adults were at work, DHS showed up at the door. They were there, because they had received a complaint about the condition of the house. I took the following day off of work, because the worker was supposed to return. I showed her the room that the three of us resided in, which was clean and organized. My one stepsister had a room upstairs also, and she had two boys. Her room was clean and organized also. And my father and step mother's room was clean as well. Now, the first level and basement of the house was another story. And to top it all off, we learned that my stepmom's soon-to-be brother-in-law, was a convicted sex offender. As soon as my one stepsister and I got our paycheck that Friday, we both put our belongings in storage and went to stay at a local motel until we could get into this housing program that the worker told us about. About two weeks before my husband, daughter, and I moved in, my stepsister and her boys settled into an apartment. She was a single parent with two children, whereas we were a two-parent household with one child. Once we got settled into our apartment, the worker came for a visit and said she didn't see any need to return. However, she had charged everyone with minor children with child abuse, and the charges wouldn't be sealed for 18 years. This way, if they ever had to be involved again, they would see this on our record. I knew that DHS would never have to come knocking on my door again in the future.

When we moved into this housing program, it opened a lot of other available programs that I otherwise wouldn't have known about. I started doing some practice tests for my GED. Living there also moved us up the list for leased housing, so we began exploring rental house options.

Jayson had applied for disability. He was at this point now dating a lady that he had met at his job. He was also seeing a psychiatrist regularly, which is how he received his diagnosis of schizophrenia which he started taking medication for. He and the mother had their rights terminated for their daughter, along with the other three children she had. His daughter and her youngest sibling were adopted by the same family.

Chapter 19

As January of the new millennium rolled around, so did my due date for my son. I was due on January 6th. However, when that date arrived, I hadn't even had a single contraction, and I had been measuring 40 for about the past four weeks. This baby was definitely larger than my daughter, and he had run out of room in my stomach. So, on January 7th, I drank a tablespoon of castor oil, because I had heard that it could help start labor. That night my stomach just had a lot of gas bubbles in it. On the morning of the 8th, when I woke, I started doing housework. As I did, I noticed that I was having pains in the lower part of my abdomen that would hold for about 30 seconds and then release. There was no doubt that they were indeed contractions. I timed the amount of time in between, and they were about ten minutes apart. I didn't want to be sent home from the hospital the way I had with my first pregnancy, so I started some laundry.

My husband woke up about two hours after me. I told him that I had a load of laundry in the dryer and asked him if he would go downstairs to grab them. I also told him that I had been having contractions since I had woken up. He asked if I wanted him to start another load. Well, by this time the contractions were about seven minutes apart, and they had begun to intensify. I told him that after he grabbed the laundry, I thought we should load our daughter's bag as well as mine into the car, and start making our way towards the hospital. By the time I had picked up my friend who was supposed to be in the delivery room with me and dropped my daughter off, another two hours had passed. When we arrived at the hospital, the contractions were now five minutes apart. When they checked me upstairs in labor and delivery, I was 4 centimeters dilated, so they admitted me and started Pitocin to intensify the contractions to help progress the labor. Things were progressing well, they had broken my water, and I was now 8.5 centimeters dilated. All of a sudden, a couple of nurses came rushing back into my room, and they said they needed me on my side, as they tried to stimulate the baby that was still inside me. Apparently, his heart rate had dropped to an unsafe level. Things improved, well, for a short time anyway, until they came rushing in again. They checked again to see if I was fully dilated yet, but nothing had changed yet. They explained to me that they were going to start an epidural for precautionary reasons, just in case we had to rush in for an emergency cesarean. After I received the epidural, the staff came rushing back in again. This time, they said if his heart rate dropped one more time, that we would be heading to the operating room. By this time, I had been cut, and was now 9.5 centimeters dilated, so they said they wanted me to push with the next contraction. They wanted to monitor how the baby would tolerate me pushing. They had kicked my friend out of the delivery room for precautionary reasons. Instead, there were three doctors and at least four nurses in the room. Once I started pushing, the baby's heart rate went back up and stayed up. I only pushed for a half-hour until my son was welcomed into the world. He was born on January 9th, 2000, at 12:30 am, weighing in at 9 lbs 1.5 oz and was 21 inches long. He was named Johnathon.

I was exhausted after giving birth to my son, and I knew my daughter would be brought to meet her new baby brother in just a couple more hours. So when the nurses asked if I would like for them to take him to the nursery so I could rest for a while, I agreed. However, he wasn't in there for long, as I was going to try to breastfeed him. After a little while of trying to get him to latch on, I asked them just to bring me a bottle of formula instead. After I fed him the two-ounce bottle, he and I both slept for at least three hours. That would have been because our first visitor had arrived. It was Uncle Jayson who came to meet his new nephew. He came bearing gifts: two Ty Beanie Babies for me, a teddy bear, and a beautiful white seal, and I believe three Ty Beanies for his new nephew. I know one was a lizard, one a monkey, and I don't recall what the third one was, but Jayson hung them on the side of his nephew's little bed. Jayson stayed for quite a while, getting acquainted with his new nephew. Our next visitors arrived while Jayson was still there. This time it was my friend and her family, and my very busy, bossy, and sassy two-year-old. For the last six months of my pregnancy, my best friend and I were pregnant together. She welcomed her second child into the world three months and 9 days after my son was born. My daughter didn't seem super interested in her new baby brother. She just wanted to mess with things and climb all over me. They didn't stay super long, as my daughter was so active. I gave her a big hug, kissed her, and told her that I loved her and I would see her tomorrow, and then the following day, she could come home with me, daddy, and her new brother. Two days later, we picked up our daughter and headed home with our new bundle of joy. It took a bit of time for my very demanding two-year-old to get used to sharing her Mommy's time with her baby brother. Mom quickly learned that she had to strap the baby in his seat at all times, because on at least two occasions when I had to go into the bedroom or bathroom for something quick, I walked back out to the living room and she had picked her brother up. When she saw me both times, she would just drop him onto the floor. I learned extremely fast how to manage a newborn and a toddler. I remember another day, I was sitting in the middle of the sofa, and had the baby laying up against the back of the couch on the cushion next to me. Angelica was standing on the floor in front of the cushion her brother was on, and she was leaning over his cushion playing with his little hands with her own still tiny little hands. I glanced back at the television as I was listening to a story on the news. All of a sudden Johnathon started screaming. I looked back over and within the 20 seconds that I had looked away, she had bitten her brother's hand enough to almost break the surface of the skin. I asked her why she bit her brother and told her that it wasn't nice to bite. And showed her that she had given him an owie on his hand. I then put her in a timeout. Over the next six months or so, by the third time she had bitten her brother, I grabbed her arm and bit her. In saying that, I didn't leave any marks and hadn't actually bit her very hard at all, just enough to lightly pinch the skin and make it sting a little bit. I didn't know what else I could do to get her to stop biting her brother. After that day, she never bit her brother again.

By February 2000, when my son was about a month old, I took the test for my GED, and passed it with flying colors. Not too bad for a ninth grade dropout. I had the potential to go far in my education, I just wasn't given the opportunity nor had the encouragement to live my life to the fullest and keep up with my studies. Nor could I handle the torment from my peers any longer. Depression, low self-esteem, and secluding myself away from people as often as I could. I would also inflict pain on myself by putting cuts on different areas of my body. I pretty much hated myself for a very long part of my life. I truly believed that I was ugly and fat (which, let's just confirm, I had always been a bigger girl since I started my period and had developed at the age of 10), and that nobody loved me, or wanted to be around me. I even believed that I deserved the awful ways that people treated me because there was obviously something wrong with me. For several years, after I gave birth, however, I was able to put my past on a top shelf in a closet, as if it didn't exist. Because two young children can keep a mother busy from before dawn and until after dusk.

On March 1st of 2000, we were approved for leased housing, and we moved into a three-bedroom house. At this time, my husband was working at the airport in the restaurant as a cook. And I was still working at Pearson Education.

I had recently told my husband that I wanted him to start helping with the middle-of-the-night bottle feeding. I explained to him that it wasn't fair that I had to get up every night when our daughter was a baby, and had now for the first couple of months since our son was born. Let's just say that didn't last past the very first night after I made him get up. When I woke him and told him that our son was crying and was gonna need to be fed, he stomped into the children's room and then down the stairs. I could hear him downstairs slamming cabinets and being grouchy with our baby. At that point, I went downstairs and told him that our son was only two months old and didn't understand his yelling at him or telling him that he was getting the bottle. I told him to go back to bed, and I finished feeding and changing my handsome little boy before putting him into his crib and going back to bed myself.

About a month after we got settled into our new house, we decided to host a party so that our friends and family could come see our house. Our guests weren't asked to bring anything, just themselves. We bought food, drinks, and alcohol. Well let's just say that we would not repeat having everyone over like that again, because a total of $170 was stolen from us that night.

By September 2000, I had come to the realization that my children's father really wasn't going to help me much with the kids' care and such. So I scheduled an appointment and had my tubes cut, tied, and burnt. At this point, I had the best of both worlds, one girl and one boy, and I had decided many years before having children that I didn't want children by multiple fathers, Since I had grown up in a home where we all had different dads.

On Halloween, we celebrated Angelica's third birthday, and shortly after that, it was Christmas, new year, and then Johnathon's 1st birthday.

Chapter 20

At the beginning of 2001, we started doing some research on our new desktop computer that the in-laws had bought us for Christmas. My husband was finally told his birth name. So, we just typed his full name and then hit search. We were surprised to see that there was a phone number listed under the exact same name as his. So I said to him, "This is what you have been wanting for a really long time, and now we have the phone number that the worst they could do is reject you."

He dialed the number that we found online. The voice of an elderly lady answered the phone. My husband explained the situation to her about how he had been adopted when he was young, and then he told her about learning his birth name recently, which happened to be the same name as her late husband's. This woman he was having a conversation with turned out to be his grandmother. She gave him the phone number of his birth mother. It took him a short time to muster up the courage to place the call. When he did call his birth mother, he learned that she lived near Ames in Story County. So I said to him, "This is what you have always wanted, let's take tomorrow off of work and go meet her." She lived less than three hours from where we lived.

He called her on the phone again and asked if he could come the following day to meet her, and she agreed. The following day, we got some stuff together for the kids like an extra change of clothes, diapers, sippy cups, and snack and drink items to keep them happy on the road trip.

We finally arrived at the place where his mother lived. The woman inside this house, his mother, held the key to all of the unanswered questions that he had always contemplated and pondered over in his mind. We went inside and met her and her husband. We learned that she also had two daughters, which meant that he did have biological siblings. However, his mother said that when they learned of a brother, they were both angry and didn't want to meet him because they didn't want to share their mom. So, they had left the house earlier that day before we arrived.

Now there were some things that she said when the question came up about why she had given him up for adoption. She didn't just come right out and bluntly say why, however, I caught on to what she was saying. But my husband on the other hand, didn't catch what she was trying to say without saying it. Turned out, she had been raped by her father and that's how he was conceived. That's the reason she had given him up. She couldn't handle seeing her father every time she looked at her child.

I had the background of my own childhood. However, it didn't change how I felt about him or my children. Granite, had I known how he was conceived before we had children, I might have decided against having them due to the fear of unknown. I had heard that a lot of the time when children are conceived between blood relatives that it could cause the child to have deformities, which is exactly why I had spent two years punching myself in my stomach in fear of conceiving a child by my brother.

She made it fairly clear that she didn't want a relationship with him. At least he had the answers he'd longed for his whole life —Or did he?

After we got home and had put the kids to bed, he and I were talking about the events of the day.

And I said to him, “I know it was tough hearing how you were conceived, but I want you to know that it doesn’t change the way I feel about you or our children.” “What do you mean?” he asked. “Did you not hear how she said that she had conceived you? Did you not hear who she said your father was?” I asked him. “No,” he replied. I then said to him, “What she was trying to tell you, is that her father raped her and that’s how she got pregnant with you. That’s why she gave you up for adoption, because every time she looked into your face, she felt as though she was looking at her father.”

He didn’t believe what I had just told him, so he called one of his mother’s sister. Let's just say this woman doesn’t sugar coat things. She blatantly confirmed what I had just told him. He hung up the phone and ran into the kitchen. He was in tears, and kept screaming “NO.” Before I reached the kitchen, I could hear the faucet running. When I entered the kitchen, I saw he had grabbed the scouring pad from the sink and was scouring his arm. I said to him, “Stop, what are you doing?” “I feel so gross in my skin,” he replied. “It's not your fault,” I said to him. “It doesn’t change who you are, nor does it change how I feel about you.” It took considerable effort to convince him to stop trying to scrub his skin off.

While I still loved him, the news that he had learned changed him. He hated himself because he was a product of incest. Unfortunately, it also altered how he felt about our son. You see, my son shares the same birth month as me, has brown eyes like mine, and a slightly darker complexion—also like me. However, he looks just like his father. So, in a sense, he resented his son because he was a direct replica of himself.

This not only devastated him but also began to strain our relationship. He was grouchy all the time, and never wanted to go anywhere or do anything with the kids and me. He just wanted to give up on life. I tried to encourage him to seek counseling, but he wouldn't.

One night, as we went to bed, he began to initiate sex. I told him, "I don't want to have sex tonight. I'm exhausted." It quickly became obvious that he was unhappy with my response; he jumped out of bed and began stomping around, cursing, and slamming doors. At this point, I said to him, "Fine, just do whatever you want," and I lay in our bed with my head to the side. You see, as a result of my childhood, I have this ability to turn my head to the other side with a male on top of me, and mentally be somewhere else.

That being said, the fact that my husband—the man whose name I had taken and for whom I had borne children—could climb on top of me in that state, as I lay there completely still until he was finished, made him, in my mind and heart, no different from all the other terrible people who had climbed on me throughout my childhood.

About a week later, I told him that I was no longer in love with him. How could he not realize that, in my eyes, he had committed the greatest betrayal he could ever have done to me?

As the year progressed, my husband was still working at the airport, for the most part. When he wasn't at work, he spent most of his time in front of the TV, until eventually he would go to bed.

We stayed together for the sake of our kids. Time flew by, and the children were growing quickly. My husband was still working at the café in the airport during the 9/11 terrorist attacks. It was a very scary and uncertain time for everyone.

Christmas this year was a little better than the previous years, as my son was almost two years old. However, after he opened his first toy, he didn't care about opening the other gifts, so his sister assisted him with tearing the wrapping paper off the rest of his gifts. That Christmas, I also purchased a man's ring from Jayson and paid to have it resized to fit my father. I had gotten the gift for my father since his birthday was also on Christmas Day. Altogether, it cost me about $300. I wrapped it in around 10 different-sized boxes. However, a couple of months after Christmas, I asked him where the ring was. He told me that someone had stolen it from his nightstand. I'm almost certain that's not what happened—I'm convinced it ended up at the pawn shop. Needless to say, that was the last gift I ever bought for him. I had put a lot of effort, money, and thought into that gift, and it really hurt that it meant so little to him that he got rid of it so quickly.

The following year flew by quickly. The kids were growing bigger by the day and learning so much. About halfway through the year, I quit smoking cigarettes, which was one of the toughest things I've ever done. I experienced extreme mood swings, but the hardest part was the tactile addiction. I was so used to having a cigarette in my mouth and hand that I had to find other ways to cope with the urge. I chewed a lot of gum and straws. After a month, I had beaten the addiction. I was extremely proud of myself and excited about a healthier future.

As 2002 quickly wrapped up, we were looking for a new house to move into. The children were getting bigger, and we were starting to outgrow the cute little house that we had moved into almost two years ago.

Chapter 21

As the year 2003 kicked off, we were interested in a nice big rental property about three blocks from where we currently lived.

This place used to be a candy store and then a pet store from what we had been told. It was a much bigger place than where we were living, and the rent was also reasonable. So we filled out the application and waited. Around February, we decided to get a kitten from a friend of ours. She was a beautiful long-haired calico that we named Mimi and I was absolutely in love with her. I hadn't had a cat since my parents made me get rid of Sam when I was five years old.

By mid-February, we learned that we had been approved for the new rental property. The main level of the house had a screened-in porch, a living room, a dining room, a kitchen, a bedroom, a computer room, and a full bathroom. Upstairs, there was another screened-in porch, two bedrooms with beautiful French doors, another bedroom with a full bath, and a very large open room that we planned to turn into the children's playroom. We moved in on the first of March.

Shortly after settling in, we decided to get a playmate for Mimi.

The kids' dad said that he wanted to pick out the kitten this time so we went to someone's house that had free kittens. He chose an all-gray one that we named Shadow. The two kittens became fast friends.

We started going to a lot of auctions and garage sales to find items to fill up our house, as well as find the kids outdoor toys, with summer just around the corner. By summer the children's playroom had a sofa and an entertainment center equipped with a TV, stereo, DVD player, VHS player, and some video games. We also acquired some bikes, a power wheel jeep and quad that brought lots of entertainment for our children, as well as the neighborhood children for the next couple years.

My biggest fear with the playroom is the balcony above the stairs. I was so scared that one of the children would climb up there and fall over. I made sure not to place any large furniture near the balcony, that someone could climb on to reach it. I also held each of the children up to the balcony and had them look down to see how far the bottom of the stairs was. I explained that if they were to fall, they would get very big 'owies.' Many years later, I learned that my daughter's memory of this moment was much more extreme than it actually was. She recalled being dangled over the balcony by her feet, which of course never happened. Still, I felt bad that it had scared her enough for her mind to exaggerate the situation into something that never occurred. I was just so afraid they might climb up and fall—I definitely didn't want them to be scared either.

My father and stepmother had come over at some point and asked if they could move in with us. Feeling bad, we agreed to allow them to move in and we got off of the leased housing program. The agreement that we had was that my stepmother would not try to move any of her children in. They took the bedroom on the main level. Now, with my father staying in my home, I had some concerns about him living, where my children lived. I was, however, an extremely vigilant mom. Whenever my children were awake I was also. I did talk to my children and told them that they were not allowed in Grandpa's room, and they were not allowed to sit on their grandfather's lap or anything. I would be the main key in keeping my children safe around my father. They were always within my eyesight, even when they were downstairs and around their grandfather. I had told my father when he moved in, that he was not allowed to discipline my children either. I said if they needed to be disciplined for anything, their father or I would discipline them. My father and stepmother were actually gone a lot of the time. They worked during the day and would go to the movies and to bingo and such when not at work.

In August of 2003, I decided that I wanted to go back to school. I enrolled in Accounting classes at Hamilton College. I was just going for an accounting diploma to start with. Life was busy now. With taking classes, working at Happy Joes, making sure my husband got back and forth to work everyday, and making sure the house and everything that the kids needed was done and handled. It actually felt good being in a classroom again. It had been fourteen years since I had dropped out of school in the ninth grade. School was never the issue. In fact, I loved learning at school in my younger years, and I was good at it. What I couldn't handle anymore back then was the constant daily tormenting from my peers that I dealt with from kindergarten on.

One day, during fall season, while I was outside with the kids, even with all the toys that the children had to play with, Johnathon instead just wanted to keep climbing in and out of the car. I kept encouraging him to play with toys, but he was persistent. He would climb into the passenger seat, close the door, then he would climb out and close the door, then open it and climb back in and repeat the process. Well, let's just say, one time when he climbed out and went to close the door, he placed his left hand on the car, and ended up slamming his thumb in the car door. So, off to the emergency room we went. We learned that he had broken the growth plate in his thumb. They wrapped his hand and his arm up to just below his elbow with an Ace bandage and a splint, and we had an appointment two days later on Wednesday with orthopedics to get it casted. So, he got his cast put on when we went to orthopedics and he was excited to have people start signing it. Of course, the cast wouldn't slow him down.

Two days after he had gotten his cast, we got into a car accident around 4 am while driving my husband to work. It was lightly snowing that morning, so I was driving about 10 miles under the speed limit. As I proceeded through an intersection where I had a yellow flashing light, there was a Jeep Cherokee SUV that T-boned us on the driver's side. By the time our car stopped spinning, we were up against the curb facing the opposite direction. I immediately looked over my right shoulder at my daughter. She was now awake and crying, because the impact of the accident had scared her and woke her out of her sleep. Besides that, she was uninjured. I then turned around a little further so I could see my son who was in his car seat behind me. I was mortified, screaming and panicking, as I could barely see my baby's face—completely covered in blood. I tried to open my door so I could get out and get to my baby, but my door wouldn't open. So, my husband got him out of the back seat from the passenger side as I climbed across the front seat to get out.

The woman that hit us, hadn't even attempted to stop at that stop light. She said that she didn't think she had to stop since the light was flashing. It was a red flashing light. Red means stop, whether flashing or not. How did she obtain a driver's license? It seemed like forever before the ambulance got there. Angelica wiped a little blood off of her brother's face with her pink little gloves as she was crying and said, "Please don't die Bub." It was so sad. When the ambulance arrived, they papoosed my baby on a backboard and put a neck brace on him. We all piled into the back of the ambulance and when the ambulance started moving, my back started spasming so badly that I was instantly in tears. So, they stopped the ambulance and ended up moving the backboard that held my son over to the bench seat, and then strapped me onto a backboard with a neck brace as well for precaution. On the ride to the hospital, I had my husband call Jayson. Jayson's girlfriend answered his phone and when my husband told her that we had been in an accident and that Johnathon was injured, she told him that she was going to try to wake Jayson up, but couldn't guarantee that he would wake up. Let's just say as soon as she told him about the accident and that his nephew was injured, he jumped straight out of bed and made it to the hospital before the ambulance had.

Jayson loved his nephew a lot, and Johnathon worshiped the ground his uncle walked on. Jayson stopped in to see me and how I was doing, and I asked him to go make sure his nephew was ok. Johnathon ended up with about 30 stitches on his face that day. His uncle stood there, holding his hand the whole time while singing Bob the Builder to him. He had stitches in two cuts in his left eyebrow, some in a wound in the center of his forehead, another wound by his right temple, and the last two stitches actually went in his left eyelid.

They put the last two in with no novocaine because they said it would hurt worse to numb it and then stitch it, rather than to just weave the two stitches through. He had another cut that looked like a large fishhook shape in the middle of his forehead. Thank goodness the cut wasn't any deeper, because it would have scalped my son. We were lucky that the CT scans for both of us were good. I felt a lot better since they had given me some muscle relaxers and pain meds in the emergency room.

After the accident, I started stressing to my husband that I wanted and needed him to start working towards getting his license because it wasn't fair to have to drag the kids out of bed and out of the house at 3ish every morning to drive him to work. The fact of the matter was, he had never had a license, and hadn't ever been in trouble for driving without a license or anything; he just had no enthusiasm to have a license or learn how to drive.

I wasn't willing to let this go. I could understand if maybe his license was currently suspended or something, but that just wasn't the case. I started driving him to the DOT every day that they were open, so that he could continue taking the written test until he could pass it. On several days, it would turn into an argument. Either he would start snapping when I told him, "C'mon, let's go try your written test again," or he would wait till we arrived at the DOT and say, "I forgot my ID at home." So I would say, "Well we're gonna go home, get it and come back." That always angered him more. I had gotten a minivan and told him that he could have the Ford Taurus that we had. He was very adamant about doing everything he could think of to get out of getting his license, but after about 10 times, he finally passed the written test.

And on the third attempt he passed the driving test. Finally.... This was a major relief for me. Even if he didn't do any of the household driving, or taking the kids where they needed to go, at least he could get himself to and from work.

Before the year was up, I started having a recurring dream night after night. Now this had only ever happened one other time in my life, which was the dreams I was having about my mother passing away. This time, the dreams weren't about my mother, but rather dreams about Jayson. Jayson was getting high a lot around this time, and he preferred shooting the drugs. Sometimes he was up and sometimes he was out of it. In this dream that I kept having, someone was either pounding on my door, or screaming in my ear over the phone that Jayson was dead from an overdose. One day when Jayson stopped by the house, I had a personal conversation with him. I said to him, "Jayson, you have to slow down on the drugs." "Please Jayson, I keep having these dreams that someone is contacting me screaming that you're dead from an overdose." I said, "This has only happened one other time in my life, Jayson, which was when Mom died." "Please stop," I pleaded with him as I began to sob. "Sissy, I'll never do more than I can handle," he responded.

Exactly one week later, I received that phone call that I had dreamt about over and over again. It was his girlfriend on the other end of the line, and all I got from our phone conversation was, "He's foaming at the mouth, and they're working on him." I ran out the door, jumped in my vehicle, and started driving as fast as I could across town towards Jayson's house. When I was about a half mile away from his house, I received another phone call saying that the ambulance had just left their house and was heading to the hospital.

I quickly turned back around to start my journey towards the hospital. I arrived just before the ambulance did and ran into the emergency room. They told me that it would be a little while before I'd be able to see him, because they had to stabilize him. When I was finally allowed to go back, I walked into the room, and there laid my brother with a ventilator breathing for him. The road to recovery would take a while, but at least they were able to revive him. While the future was still unsure, my brother was alive. He remained on the ventilator in a coma for a couple of days before he woke up. He apparently had overdosed on cocaine and heroin. He had vomited and aspirated on his vomit. So he now had pneumonia in his lungs. It took a few weeks for the pneumonia to get out of his lungs, however, there was some permanent damage that would now lead to a life of having to see a pulmonologist. I, on the other hand was super happy just to have my brother still here with me.

Chapter 22

A new year was upon us. Johnathon was now 4, and Angelica was 6. The kids' dad was still working at the airport, and I was still attending classes and delivering pizzas. The children's father and I seemed to be fighting a lot more these days, Mostly because he rarely ever helped me with the kids. I bathed them, and got them dressed in the morning and at night. I took them outside to play, and took them to every appointment that they had. I was exhausted trying to do everything for the kids while working and taking classes.

It had been 3 months since Jayson's overdose, when I received yet another phone call from his girlfriend screaming and crying again. Jayson had overdosed again and the paramedics were trying to revive him once more . Now, for the second time, I walked into his room in the emergency department, to see my brother hooked to a ventilator again. This time, however, he was taken to the cardiac intensive care unit. Jayson had suffered a heart attack. A day or two after he overdosed, I went to the hospital and took the children with me. They really wanted to see their uncle. As the children and I stood at the bottom of his bed, Jayson woke up. He looked at the children and me, and then looked towards the door where he saw the words "Cardiac ICU." I busted into tears. My brother was alive and conscious again. They took the ventilator off of him later that day, and so began the road to recovery again.

The stresses of everything going on, led me right back to smoking cigarettes again. It literally started with a couple drags off one of my father's cigarettes, and next thing you know, I was right back at the store buying a pack. I had made it a year and half cigarette-free.

Thankfully, Jayson's second overdose scared him bad enough that he took time to get sober. And he was spending a lot of time with his nieces and nephews. Jayson literally had seven computers and laptops hooked up at his house, so that each of the nieces and nephews had their own computer to play on when he had them all over. He's always been really good with kids, and all the kids loved him. He was the cool uncle. In my son's eyes his uncle could do no wrong. Every time he knew I was talking to his uncle he would say, "Mom, can I talk to Jay?" When I handed him the phone, the first thing he always asked his uncle was. "Are you coming over?" Their relationship was completely priceless sometimes.

One night as I was doing dishes in the kitchen, my son entered the room and said to me, "Mom, I'll be right back." "Whoa, wait a minute. What do you mean you'll be right back? Where do you think you're going?" I asked him. He said, "I'm going to get Uncle Jayson." "What do you mean you're going to get Uncle Jayson?" I asked. He responded, "I'm going to ride my bike to his house to get him." So I asked him, "Do you even know the way to your uncle's house? And how do you think you're going to get your uncle back here?" "He's going to ride on the handlebars," he said to me. I'm trying not to laugh, and thinking that I'm going to kick Jayson's ass when I see him. I said to my son, "Honey, it's 8:30 at night, there's a bunch of snow outside, you don't know the way to your uncle's house, and your uncle's fat butt isn't going to fit on your handlebars." At this point he starts crying, "But Mom, Uncle Jayson said so." I said, "Son, you're not going to your uncle's house, and I'm gonna beat him up next time I see him." He stayed mad at me for the rest of the night.

I recall another time when Jayson came over. He had his canister of chewing tobacco in his shirt pocket. Now at this point, my children couldn't say tobacco, so they called it tabasco. Johnathon asked his uncle, "What's in your pocket?" Jayson said, "It's my tabasco. Who wants some tabasco?" both of my children's hands shot straight up in the air. Jayson stomps on the floor and said loudly, "Open your mouth." Both of the children screamed and ran all the way through the house to the bathroom and locked the door. Jayson would pound on the outside of the bathroom door yelling, "Open your mouth." You could hear the kids screaming and laughing from the other side of the locked door. Then Jayson would come back in the living room, and wait for them to come back.

Before long, they reappear in the living room and they stood right in front of their uncle waving at him. Again Jayson says, "Who wants some tabasco?" Both kids instantly raise their hand again, as their uncle bellowed, "Open your mouth." The kids again scream with excitement as they run through the house again to the bathroom. Again, Jayson pounds on the locked door yelling, "Open your mouth." Once again the kids just scream in glee. Let's just say, by the third time, I was ready for Jayson to go home. Whenever Jayson was around kids, it only took about 2 minutes to have all the children wound up, and the noise level would have increased at least tenfold from what it had been before he arrived.

In August of that year, I graduated from Hamilton College with an accounting diploma. I actually ended that year with a grade point average of 3.86 —not too shabby for someone who dropped out in 9th grade. The Sad thing is that the accounting diploma didn't help me to obtain a better job, because people don't really hire for entry-level positions. And I couldn't afford another year, since I was already $8,000 in debt from the first year. At least I could say that I got my GED, and that I did attend college.

Life was seeming a little calmer with my schedule not as hectic as it was trying to juggle work, school, home, and kids. Well, it was calmer besides all the arguing and yelling that was happening daily between my husband and me. It was around this time that I started talking to my kids a lot about safe touches and bad touches. I told them that any area that is covered by a girls' bathing suit or a boys' swim trunks is private. I had my daughter hold her arms out to the side and told her to spin around in a circle. I then asked her, "Do you see how big that circle is?" and then told her that was her bubble, and she didn't have to let anyone within the space of her bubble if she didn't want them there. I then talked to the kids and told them that if anyone ever touched them where their bathing suit or swim trunks cover or asked to see them areas, or showed the kids their private area, or wanted them to touch them on their private area, they should come tell me immediately. I even told them that these kinds of people may threaten them and tell them that they will harm them or other members of our family if they told.

And I explained to them that they may even tell them that it's a secret. And I reassured my children that, if anyone ever did something bad like that to either one of them, as long as they told me, I will make sure that person never hurts them again. I also told the kids that they didn't have to give people like aunts, uncles, grandparents, cousins, etc. hugs and kisses, or handshakes, or even tell them that they love them, if it made them uncomfortable at all.

I also told them, like when uncle Jayson stops by and has a friend with him, just because Uncle Jayson knows them or because it's his friend, it doesn't give them permission to sit on that person's lap, or to be in that person's bubble.

I told them the things that I did, because this was one of the most important things. I have always believed that we need to help keep children from be sexually traumatized for the rest of their life. Communicating with your children about these situations is important in the fight to keep them safe in today's world. If I didn't talk to my children about predators, then how would they know? After someone abused them, it is too late for you to explain them what the plan was in the case that someone touched them inappropriately. Now, maybe they'll hear the threats of their predator, telling them that they'll hurt someone if they tell. What if they never tell? Even worse, imagine it keeps happening for an extended period of time, without telling you. And why? Because they didn't know that they were supposed to tell you, because you never had that conversation with them.

This is where the trauma from my childhood, and the years of being sexually assaulted would intermingle with my being a mother. I was a worrisome mother while my children were younger, and probably a little more than most people due to my history. But also, the day I gave birth to each of my children, it became my job, and promise to my children, from that very moment to protect, nurture, encourage, support, and most importantly to love them. Which meant in every single way that I could, because they didn't ask to be born, but I chose to carry them and bring them into this world. So, it's my job to always protect them. I never wanted them to experience the things that I had lived through.

In elementary school, I never let my children walk to or from school, unless maybe it was a nice day and I had decided to walk with them. To be honest, for many years, I never let them out of my site except for when they were at school. My kids never went outside to play, unless I was outside with them, so that I could keep an eye on them, even if they just wanted to play in the backyard. At this stage, I always made our house a very kid-friendly and fun place to be—kind of like the place to be. And the reason I maintained stuff like that, is because I figured that if I made our place the place where all the neighbor kids know they're welcome anytime, than I wouldn't have to worry about where my children were or who they were with, cause everyone wants to play at our house, so quite naturally that's where my children always were also. I'd allow their friends to get in my vehicle for a ride to school so they didn't have to walk in the cold or rain, but I did set rules for them to ride. First, as the adult, I needed to hear from their parent or guardian to get their verbal consent for the child to ride. Just as I wouldn't want my children to get in anyone's car without my knowledge, I wouldn't let other's children in mine.

And secondly, I don't care what they may do in their parent's cars, but my vehicle didn't start unless everyone's seatbelts were buckled. If one of the children took their seat belt off as I was driving, I would pull the car over and shut it off until that child put their belt back on.

I also, like the neighborhood mom, wanted to always keep other children safe while they were in my home. The same way as I kept mine safe. In my house, all the children know that when they got there and all the boys were upstairs hanging out, the girls would have to stay downstairs and find something to do till either the boys got bored with what they were doing and came down, or I made all the kids switch so that the boys would come downstairs to let the girls play for a while upstairs. On the occasion that all the children were upstairs at the same time, the boys would have to stay in my son's room and the girls in my daughter's room. I loved having a house full of children.

During the summer, I would buy the boxes of 100-count icees and bring the box outside once a day. Whatever children were present could choose an icee, and I always made sure to bring scissors to cut off the tops. Sometimes, some of the children would try to grab a handful, but I would quickly remind them that each child could have just one. Some would even say to me, "But my sister or my cousin," and I would tell them, "Well, since they aren't here, they don't get one this time." I would also tell them that if their siblings or cousins wanted one, they would have to bring them the next day. I was the popsicle mom during the summers.

Chapter 23

As 2005 was upon us, Angelica was now in first grade and would start second grade in the fall.

Johnathon would also be starting kindergarten in the fall. During the summer of this year, I had decided to have some family over for an evening of the adults playing cards and having a couple of drinks, while the children played upstairs. When everyone arrived that day, I sent the other children upstairs where my children were. I had said to all the adults, "Nobody is allowed upstairs besides the children and myself. If your children are upstairs and you need them for anything, I will go up and get them for you."

When they arrived, one of the adults that had come over also brought a friend of theirs. Now, I wasn't keen about this "friend" that was with them. As a matter of fact, this individual's whole look and demeanor made me uncomfortable. Everything about this person screamed "PEDOPHILE" to me. I decided that I would keep an extra close eye on this individual. At some point, I had left the table to go use the restroom and make another drink. I then joined the others back at the table. Instantly, I realized that this individual was no longer sitting at the table. I stood up and walked to the living room to see if maybe he had gone in there to maybe watch the television. When I didn't see him in the living room, I started feeling a little panicked. I quickly ran up the stairs, and since my daughter's room is the first room at the top of the stairs, I yanked her door open. As I opened the door, there this individual was. He was sitting on the floor with the girls, playing with Barbies. I was furious. I screamed at him, "What the fuck are you doing in my daughter's room? I said nobody was allowed up here except for the children and myself. Get your fucking ass back downstairs." And then I said to my daughter, "There should never be a man in your bedroom, especially someone who you don't know. You should have come downstairs immediately to tell me."

I then joined everyone else downstairs. I reiterated that there were to be no adults upstairs. We continued playing cards. Eventually, I got up to use the restroom again, and immediately once I walked back into the dining room, I instantly noticed that this individual was missing from the table again. I quickly ran up the stairs again. I flung my daughter's door open again, but he wasn't in her room this time. As I came around the entertainment center in the kids' playroom, there he was. I was beyond furious. He was laying on the floor on his left side, watching the television. Now what really upset me is that my son was laying on this person on the right side of his body. "You have two seconds to get downstairs," I yelled at him.

He quickly jumped up and headed for the stairs. I then swatted my son on his bottom, and I asked him, "Do you know that person?" "No," he responded back to me. "Mommy has told you that we don't be that close to someone you don't know." I sent him to his room. I then headed downstairs because after not once, but twice finding this person upstairs where my children were, he was not only going downstairs, but I was going to ensure he left my house.

"It's time for you to get the fuck out of my house, and don't you ever come back here," I screamed at him. Right after I told him to leave, someone spoke up and said, "Well, if he has to leave, then we…" I didn't even wait for them to finish the sentence; instead, I simply said, "Bye." I said that they better not ever bring this individual to my house ever again. Someone spoke up at that point and said, "Rose, I don't think it's really like that, he just really likes kids." "I know the fuck he does," I responded. I then decided that I was done with company for the night, and said, "As a matter of fact, it's time for everyone to leave for the night."

After I cleared out the house, I headed back upstairs to talk to my children. I told them, "The reason Mommy is so upset is because I have talked to you kids several times about stranger dangers, and more than anything, I don't want anyone to hurt either one of you." We then sat in their playroom and watched a movie before I sent them to bed for the night.

One night as I lay in my bed sleeping, I awoke with a startle. I had just heard 3-4 popping noises outside. I believed it may have been gunshots; however, I wasn't certain, as I had never heard gunshots before that in my life. I guess that's what is called some small-town girl stuff. I climbed out of bed, and as I was walking into the bathroom off of my bedroom, I heard more popping noises, another three or four of them. I was completely sure at that time that it was indeed gunfire that I had heard. As a matter of fact, as I walked back into my bedroom from the bathroom, the entire house was lit up with red and blue flashing lights. I woke my husband and told him to come downstairs with me. As we got to the bottom of the staircase, we met up with my father and stepmother. They too had been woken up from the gunshots. As we all walked out onto the screened porch at the front of the house, we quickly saw why there were flashing lights outside. Somebody had indeed been shot. As a matter of fact, the individual collapsed in the middle of the road directly in front of our home. That morning, I had gone from someone that had never heard gunshots to watching an entire crime scene investigation taking place outside.

It was fairly scary. I was glad that my children didn't wake up until after the flashing lights from the police cars had stopped. Even if they had, I would not have allowed them to look outside until at least after the body had been moved and the crime scene cleaned up a bit. However, this event had scared me enough that I was now starting to talk amongst myself and the other three adults in the house about moving.

Six days before Halloween, as I was on a delivery from my job, while exiting a customer's stairs, I stepped down off the bottom stair with my left foot. When I did, my left ankle twisted, just as it had on many other occasions since I had broken it when I was a child. Unfortunately, my right foot still had to come down from the bottom step. When my left ankle twisted, it made me come down really hard with the right foot, as it had made me fall when the left one went out. So, when the right foot came down from the bottom step, it rolled inward.

As I was now completely on the ground at the bottom of my customer's stairs, I was in excruciating pain as I tried to get back on my feet. Tears were stinging my eyes. I couldn't seem to stand up because I couldn't bear any weight on either one of my feet. I crawled across the customer's driveway to the driver's door of my delivery vehicle and somehow managed to climb into the driver's seat. Both of my ankles were swelling at a very rapid rate. Somehow, I managed to drive back to my job.

When I pulled up behind the building to the door that employees enter through, I forced myself to stand up. I half crawled my way through the back hall to the dining room and sat down in a booth. The only person that I could think to call who had a vehicle and could come pick me up and take me to the hospital was my father. I was completely in tears at this point. The pain was absolutely unbearable. I yelled for my manager and explained to him what had happened and that I had to leave work to go to the hospital.

When my father arrived, my manager helped me outside and into my father's car. As I got into the car, I noticed my children's father was also in the car. When we arrived at the emergency room, my husband grabbed a wheelchair and pushed me inside and told me to call home when I was finished. It turned out that I had severely sprained my left ankle, broken the right one, and as a result of the right foot rolling inward with the fall, a tendon that was attached to the smaller bone in the back of my calf had actually ripped a chunk of the bone off of the rest of it. That caused me to bleed on the inside of my leg, which then moved down and collected in my right foot. It was extremely dark purple from my large toe, all the way around the back of my ankle to my little toe. The blood that had collected in my foot was at least an inch thick all the way around.

Thankfully, we had a recliner at that time because there was no way I would be able to get upstairs to my room. I took a lot of pain pills and slept a lot over the first couple of days. Sometimes I would even have one of the children on my lap watching cartoons as I slept. Every time I dropped the footrest of the recliner, and the blood was able to flow back down to my foot, the pain was so bad that it instantly brought tears to my eyes. I did have an E boot on my right leg and foot. I had to keep one of the dining room chairs next to the recliner because every time I needed to get up and use the restroom, I had to lean most of my weight on the back of that chair and slowly slide it through the living room, dining room, down the hall, and into the restroom. The worst part about it all is that I got hurt on October 25th, which means six days before my daughter's birthday. Thankfully, I was always way ahead of schedule and organized when it came to birthday parties, so the basement was already set up for her party. I wouldn't be able to make it down the basement stairs, but I did get down on the living room floor and scooted on my bottom until I made it to the top of the basement stairs, which I would have to coordinate from there.

We actually had her birthday party a day or two before Halloween, because we always had her parties on the weekend before Halloween, so it was easier for people to attend. Unfortunately, it was during this birthday party that our beloved calico cat named Mimi had apparently escaped while someone was entering or leaving our house that day. Angelica, for probably a month after, wanted to walk around the neighborhood daily calling for Mimi, even taking our other cat Shadow along while looking for her, thinking that if Mimi could smell or hear Shadow, she would come out from wherever she was. It was extremely hard for her to just accept that she was gone and wasn't coming back home.

On the day of Halloween, as I started to get my children dressed in their costumes, I started giving my husband suggestions on where he should take the children for trick-or-treating. He said to me, "Rose, I told you I'm not going with the kids trick-or-treating this year; I told you I was staying home and passing out candy." He had indeed said that at the end of Halloween the previous year. I, however, just assumed that since I was incapacitated this year, with him being the second parent, he would step up to the plate and take care of things when I wasn't able to. I asked him, "So what, are you going to tell your daughter that she can't go trick-or-treating on her birthday?" "Rose, I told you I'm staying home this year," he said again. I was so tired of his detachment to be engaged and involved in his children's lives, but I wasn't going to have this argument with him. It took me a half-hour just to get outside to where my van was. I was in so much pain, but I wasn't going to let my children down. After I got into my van, I took the E-boot off of my right foot. It brought tears to my eyes every time I had to push on the gas and brake pedals, but I saw to it that my injury and my husband being an ass didn't ruin my children's night. I wasn't able to walk with them, but I was able to follow along with them in my van as they went door to door. At the end of the day, my children went trick-or-treating.

As time went on, I was starting to develop hatred toward the man that I married. We seemed to fight on almost a daily basis these days. We moved out of that house in March of the next year, and my father and stepmother ended up moving in with one of her children.

Chapter 24

The next house that we moved into was quite a bit smaller than the last one, but we didn't have as many neighbors, it had a garage and a gas fireplace, and the rent was cheaper. It was on a huge double lot, at the end of a street, and the house sat behind the garage near the alley. So our house was pretty much lined up with our neighbor's garages. Shortly before we made this move, my husband started slacking off at his job and calling in a lot. He had a tendency to cause his blood sugars to go high or low whenever he wanted to get out of stuff, or if he didn't want to work, or if he was at work and wanted to go home for the rest of the day. In fact, they had now cut his hours at the airport. He overall just seemed detached, unenthused about anything, and had become quite lazy. So I went back to work that year as a temp at Pearson, while still keeping my job doing pizza delivery. I had to work two jobs to compensate for his income decrease.

My daughter was now in second grade, and her brother was officially in kindergarten. About halfway through the school year, when I was called to my son's school for a conference, it was suggested to me that I take my son to the University of Iowa hospitals for an evaluation. So I scheduled an appointment. It was an entire day of testing when we went to the appointment. Once all of the testing was finalized, my son's diagnosis was Tourette's, ADHD, OCD, cognitive disorder (which means problems with reasoning and planning, and common sense skills), conduct disorder (anger disorder), and disorder of written expression (which meant he would transpose letters and numbers, or write them backwards). Of course, recommended treatment was medications. And so the fun began of starting and stopping meds to find the right combination. On the last day of kindergarten, I dropped my son off at school, and by the time I arrived back home, the school was calling. They told me that as the children had sat down for circle time, they had witnessed my son having a seizure. I immediately rushed back to the school to pick him up to take him to the hospital. He was diagnosed with epilepsy. Not surprising, since I too had epilepsy.

One night as I lay in my bed asleep, my husband woke me up and told me that he was having chest pains. I asked him if he wanted me to call an ambulance, or if he wanted me to drive him. He said that he would just drive himself and would call me once they gave him an answer. When he came back home, he didn't have a direct answer, rather an appointment for later in the day to go to the cath lab. After that appointment, he was admitted to the hospital, as he would need to have double bypass surgery in two days. They said two of his arteries were about 95% clogged. The day that he had surgery, when I took the children to see their dad, we stopped at the gift shop at the hospital, where I let the kids pick out a vase with a couple of flowers in it and also a balloon for their dad. The balloon that I had bought him said, "Some people will do anything for attention." Not saying that he had surgery for attention, but simply because I was so fed up with so many things with him. It was always his diabetes this, or diabetes that. Granted he had diabetes since the age of seven, so he did know what he needed to do as far as diet and such to better control his diabetes. He simply chose not to take his insulin or to not eat like he should to make his sugars high or low.

As this was around the time that the kids would be starting school for the next school year, his needing this surgery put even more of a strain on our finances. One day I stopped at a station to put gas in my vehicle and decided to spend $2 on two one-dollar scratch tickets. Much to my surprise when I scratched the second one, I had won $300. Let me just say this couldn't have happened at a better time, considering that I needed to get the kids' shoes, outfits, and school supplies to start the new school year with. Blessings do come sometimes in life at just the right time. This was definitely one of those times. Just one less worry on my mind. With my husband having surgery, there were now more responsibilities that were solely mine for a while. Which means all the housework and all the lawn care on top of working two jobs and keeping up with everything the kids needed as well as everything they had going on like after-school activities, appointments, and conferences. On a daily basis, my days began at around 5:00 am, and I didn't stop moving until I finally was able to lay down for the night at around 11:00 pm. I was exhausted all the time. I understand, as I have had several broken bones throughout my life as well as multiple surgeries, that when bones are broken, or with surgeries, it does take a while for the bones or injuries to heal. However, at six months and well beyond that, every time that I would ask my husband to do something, his answer was always that he couldn't due to his surgery. I know that he had completely healed from his surgery and in fact should be feeling so much better considering his arteries were no longer clogged. For the entire year, I had to take care of all the shoveling and mowing. As if my schedule wasn't jam-packed already. My anger and hatred for the man I married seemed to increase by the day. We had entered into this partnership together knowingly and willingly, but it's not exactly a partnership when only one member is an active participant.

My husband ended up getting fired from his job at the airport as a result of his attendance. I struggled to get him to search for new employment. Often, when I would drive him places to apply for employment, I would indeed have to fill out the application for him because he wouldn't put much information on the application, or he would just put for reason for leaving previous jobs, fired, or quit. Or where it asked, "Do you have restrictions that could prevent you from performing the job functions?" he would write, "I have diabetes." He truly didn't want to find employment, and half the time my trying to drive him around to apply places generally resulted in another argument. I was so sick of his laziness and lack of enthusiasm.

Since trying to help him find employment wasn't going the best, and with my very limited amount of free time to drive him to places (because he wouldn't drive himself), I was tired of fighting and arguing with him, so I just buried myself in as much work as I could. I was now working all overtime offered to me at Pearson and delivering pizza virtually every night of the week. Since I had to work so much, I would ask him to take care of certain chores at home, but that didn't go well either. I would come home after working twelve to thirteen hours in a day, and I would ask him, "So did you do the laundry today?" Or if I had said to him, "I thought I asked you to do the dishes today," he seemed to always respond with, "I forgot." I then, before I could relax or go to bed for the night, would have to complete the tasks that he neglected to accomplish. Daily I was beyond exhausted, frustrated, and beyond missing my children. I generally only had about an hour to an hour and a half to spend with the kids in between jobs. I hated being away from them as much as I was, but I didn't have another option. The bills still needed to be paid.

Unfortunately, the housing company that we had gone through to rent the house that we were currently renting would only let us sign a 3-month lease at a time. Every three months when we would renew the lease, they would raise the rent. It had come to the point that I was now paying more in rent for this house than the last one. It in fact was becoming more than I could afford with both of my jobs. So as 2007 was wrapping up, the search for our next rental house was underway since income tax time was right around the corner. It turns out the owner of the housing company that we had been renting from was arrested a couple of months later and charged with multiple counts of fraud.

Chapter 25

As 2008 had began, the house searching was in full swing. We ended up finding a house on the other side of town. We would move in on the first of March. This was a nice-sized three-bedroom house with a nice-sized living room, dining room, kitchen, and computer room, and a full basement. It also had a nice-sized backyard. We ended up getting a lot of use out of the backyard. We had a tetherball pole. And as the weather warmed, we also got a fire pit, a patio set and we put a pool up for the children. As the summer neared, so did the looming threat of upcoming flooding in Cedar Rapids. In July of 2008, the Cedar River had grown over its banks. In about a week, the river had swollen so much that it flooded entire neighborhoods, up to ten blocks on both sides of the river.

The night before we were evacuated from our home, the floodwaters were five blocks from our street. I said to my husband, "It's inevitable that the water is coming. We need to start moving stuff to higher levels." I wanted to get all of the important things and things that can't be replaced, such as photos, moved up to the top level of the house. I also wanted to move the washer and dryer up from the basement to the main level. Due to my husband's laziness to even get himself off the couch, he had responded, "Rose there's no way that the flood is going to make it all the way to our street." "No, it's definitely coming, will you please just help me?" I asked him. "Rose, I told you the water isn't going to make it this far," he said again. "Whatever, I'll just do what I can by myself," I said back to him. I managed to get all the things that I needed off the main level of the house at least. I just couldn't get the washer and dryer out of the basement by myself. The next morning as we woke and came down to the main level of the house, all of a sudden, all you could hear was water starting to pour into the basement. I said to him, "I told you yesterday that we should have gotten the washer and dryer out of the basement, but no, you insisted the water wasn't gonna get this far. Now damn it, hurry and help me get them out of the basement before they actually get ruined." We ended up having to stand and walk in about three inches of feces flooded water to finally get the washer and dryer out of the basement. Almost immediately after we finished moving the appliances, there was a knock at the front door. It was the National Guard and they were there to inform us that we had to evacuate our house. So we gathered up our pets, as well as a little bit of clothes and hygiene products for everyone. My vehicle was across the street on a little bit of an elevated part of a parking lot. By the time we left our home that morning, I was walking in water up to my thighs. By later that afternoon, they were actually docking rescue boats off of our street. In order to get across town to my step sister's house, with three of the exits closed due to flood water, we spent three hours on the interstate in bumper to bumper traffic. To be honest, it was extremely overwhelming and quite terrifying.

Since we would be staying with my brother or at my friend's house, we had to take our animals to the local community college. They were caring for pets of everyone that had been displaced from the flood. Every animal that was cared for at the college received booster vaccines as well as was microchipped. It was definitely a relief and blessing that they were caring for these animals. It just took another worry off of many families in which some were looking for temporary housing while others had lost everything they owned. It was truly amazing the way the community pulled together to help one another. Just as quickly as the flood water came up, it also receded fairly quickly. About three days after we had been evacuated, we were able to get our first look at the amount of damage to our home, as well as we needed to grab some clothing and hygiene things that we had forgotten when we had been in a rush to vacate. Fortunately, the water never reached the main level of the house, so the water had been contained to just our basement. We were extremely lucky, as many families would now have to start over after losing their entire homes and everything that they owned. I was heartbroken for so many residents of our city. As we were gathering items that we needed, I kept hearing what sounded like a kitten meowing. It took a little while to figure out where the sound was coming from. Just as I suspected, it was indeed a kitten that I was hearing. The kitten only appeared to be about two or three weeks old. I wasn't sure at first what I would do with the kitten, since we didn't even have our animals at that time. We called the local college that was housing everyone's pets and explained to them that we had found a tiny kitten inside our home when we had stopped to see the damage. They informed me that I could bring the kitten to them and they would put it in with a nursing mother cat.

Even though the water had only affected the basement, we wouldn't be able to return home until the landlord had cleaned everything up and power washed the basement. The furnace and hot water heater would both need to be replaced. I called the landlord two weeks after the flood, and he had said that everything was looking good, but it would still be a couple of days until they could get the new hot water heater installed. He said that if I was okay with staying back in my home without the water heater, then he was okay with us returning home.

I didn't have an issue with going home without the hot water heater. This wasn't the first time that I had to rough it. I would simply heat pans of water on the electric stove for bathing purposes for my family. More than anything, I just wanted to be home where I felt safe and relaxed.

A couple of days after we returned home, it was raining fairly hard, and as we didn't have downspouts on the corners of the house, I actually went outside with my shampoo bottle and washed my hair in the rainwater. That just meant less water that would need to be heated on the stove. Besides, it was July, so the rain felt amazing. Why not use a natural resource? Just one less pan of water I had to heat on the stove.

Chapter 26

Life was finally getting back to some kind of normalcy after the flood. We had bought the kids a new pool for the backyard, and the water was finally warm enough for us to be able to use it. So the kids and I were in the pool one afternoon just swimming around and playing, while my husband was rinsing things off with the hose. One of my cousins, who actually lived across the alley from us walked into the back yard, and there was some man walking with her. I didn't pay much attention, because I was having fun with my children. She said to me, "Rose, do you know who this is?" "No," I responded back, nor did I really care, until she said his name. Now the name that she said, I hadn't heard in 20 years. It was the cousin that had sexually assaulted me 23 years prior, when I was 11. The one that had been my most traumatizing experience amongst all of the sexual abuse that I endured as a child.

As I heard the name, I instantly froze. Tears immediately stung my eyes. I was trembling, my legs were shaky, and my stomach hurt so bad that I was fighting the urge to throw up. All the memories of that awful night 23 years ago came rushing back to me. As I tried to keep my composure, I said to my daughter, "Angelica, I need you to do something for me, okay?" "Okay," she responded back. "I need you to lower yourself down into the water until the water is at your neck," I said to her. "Why mom?" she asked. "Angelica, please don't ask questions. Please just do what I ask you." "Okay Mommy," she said back. "Please stay there until I tell you," I said to her. She nodded back in response. My mind started racing, and it got harder to keep my legs under me. I was fighting to keep the tears in, because I didn't want to worry the children. I stood with my back towards the direction of my cousin in an attempt to block the view of my children.

The realization comes to mind that my daughter is the exact sweet tender age that I had been twenty-three years prior. After about 5 minutes, which actually seemed like a lifetime, I finally heard my cousin say, "Goodbye, Rose," as the two of them exited the backyard. I waited about another five minutes just to be sure that they were gone. Then I said to the kids, "We're gonna go inside." Thankfully, neither of them questioned or resisted going inside, because if I tried to get any more words out at that moment, I would have burst into tears. I told both of the children to let me get out first, and I quickly wrapped them both in towels as they were climbing out. I didn't want this man to see any part of my children.

When we went inside, the kids both went to their rooms to change into pajamas, and I told them to drop their wet clothes at the top of the basement stairs. I just needed to be alone for a minute. I closed myself in the bathroom to change out of my swim clothes, and the tears just flowed out. While I was trying to get the tears to stop, I all of a sudden remembered that the doors were unlocked downstairs. My mind was racing again as I was feeling extremely panicked. "What if he just walked into my house, and is down there with the kids?" I thought to myself. I went running down the stairs and first locked the front door, and thankfully my husband had finished what he had been doing outside and was now inside, so I locked the back door as well. The kids and I curled up on the couch and watched a movie before I took them upstairs to tuck them in their beds.

My husband was so not in tune with me and didn't notice or just didn't comment or question my change in demeanor. Nothing else was spoken of that day. That is until the following week. The children and I had gone to visit Uncle Jayson for a while one afternoon. All of a sudden there was a knock at the door, and Jayson's friend, who was also visiting that day, said, "Jayson, ***** is at the door." There was that name again. As soon as I heard his name, I lost it. I instantly went into a full-blown panic attack, bawling and screaming, "Please don't let him in here, Jayson. Please, my babies are here." I couldn't control the fear and rage I felt inside me this time. I was again trembling, and my stomach hurt really bad, and I felt extremely dizzy as the tears continued to roll down my face.

Jayson stepped outside for a brief moment before rejoining the children and me inside. When he came back in, he looked at me and said, "Sissy, what the fuck?" It took me a while to catch my breath enough to actually speak, and that was when I told him what had happened on that horrific night so many years ago. That was the first time that I had told anyone about what he had done to me. In fact, I told him about all of our cousins that were involved. I had lived for all those years with the demons that haunted my mind and soul from all the sexual abuse that I was made to endure for seven grueling years as a young girl.

Even though Jayson was my brother, and we had grown up within the same household, there was a lot that had happened to me that Jayson had no idea about. However, he had been in and out of group homes and treatment facilities so much that he seemed to be out of the home more than he was there. He was shocked when I had told him how many family members had actually been involved. There was so much that he didn't know, but in fairness, he had been gone a lot, and since our mother had passed, it was hard to find a time when Jayson was sober enough to even remotely carry on a conversation as such with him. It did feel nice to finally tell someone, especially someone that loves me. Jayson was mean to me a lot when we were children, but I still always clung to him and looked up to him in a way. And I have to say, he's the only one that's been there with me consistently since the day I came home from the hospital the year I was born. I think the hardest realization that I had to come to where he's concerned is that I can't save my brother from himself when it comes to all the drug abuse. All I could do is love him and be there to support him through whatever he was going through with addiction.

Thankfully I never crossed paths with that cousin again. However, after the day that I had revealed to Jayson about our cousins, curiosity sparked my interest to look up the cousin's criminal record. I had heard twenty years prior, after my mother had passed, that he had been locked up for killing someone. However, that wasn't the case at all. He had spent the past 20 years in prison on charges of rape and sodomy. That wasn't a shock to me at all; it just angered me that the family had lied to protect his name. I know I was invited to a family gathering for Christmas that year, in which I declined. I told my auntie that I have enough love and respect for her to not bring that to her house. Because, if he even slightly turned his head in the direction of the door as I walked in with my children, that would be 100% justification enough for me to slice his throat. My auntie was upset when I told her that we would not be attending that year since he would be there. I was told that he did his time for what he had done and that

I need to leave the past in the past. After I still declined the invitation, my auntie didn't speak to me for the next six months, but that was okay with me, because I knew I had made the right decision for everyone involved. In fact, he hadn't been in Cedar Rapids long when the Federal Marshals apprehended him on new charges of the same. I hope they don't ever let him out again, and I hope he rots in prison for all the people that he has hurt.

Crazy enough, it was also around this time that people had been saying that our oldest brother had been reaching out to them to try to get in contact with Jayson and me and had also been trying to get in contact with the five children that he had helped create here in the state of Iowa. However, since the incident that was discovered by Jayson pertaining to a niece and nephew the year he disappeared, none of his children had any interest in meeting him again after all these years, and especially after learning about who he really was and the things he had done. In fact, each one of them will still say to this day that that is not their father. However, since his number had surfaced after all those years, I had an overwhelming urge to contact him. Not because I wanted to get reacquainted or anything like that, but because I wanted to confront him after all these years about the stuff in our past as well as confront him about the situation with his daughter. It took a couple of weeks to muster up the courage to place the call. Jayson was extremely upset that I was gonna contact him and in fact said to me, "That motherfucker will never hear my voice again, and if I ever see him, I'm gonna wrap my hand around his throat, and I'm not letting go until he stops moving." In fact, Jayson had told his therapist and psychiatrist so many times that if he ever sees his brother that he will kill him, that authorities here in Iowa had gotten in contact with Florida authorities to get a message to our oldest brother that if he ever comes back to Iowa, there is a threat on his life. Apparently, there's a law called the "right to know" law, in which they tell a person that there's a threat on their life. I had never heard of anything like this before.

When I finally mustered up the courage and had played over and over in my mind what I wanted to say to him, I sat down one day while the kids were in school and dialed his number. A female answered the phone, and I introduced myself as being his sister and told her that I needed to speak with him. She said he was gone at the moment, working, and that I could call back in the evening. And so that's what I did. When he answered the phone, he said, "Oh my God, Rose, I'm so glad to hear from you," and I could hear in his voice that he was crying. I asked him if I was on speakerphone or if anyone else was listening to our conversation, and he said no, that he was the only one on the phone. I said, "Good, because I didn't call today to catch up and get reacquainted; I really called because I have a few things that I need to say to you. I want you to know that I am still, at the age of 34, extremely fucked up as a result of what you, among others, did to me when we were younger. And do you know that you have never apologized to me for any of it, much less even admitted to it?" I guess I was hoping that he had gotten help and had changed. But that obviously wasn't the case, because he responded to me with, "What are you talking about? Nothing ever happened after I was put in a foster home when I was seven." I could feel the anger and rage inside me starting to boil over. "Unbelievable, he's still denying things after all these years," I thought to myself. Then I said to him, "Who the fuck are you lying to? Seriously, it's just the two of us on the phone, so who are you lying to?" And I brought up specifics including but not limited to, when I was 12, and he slid notes with pictures under my bedroom door asking me to leave my door unlocked so he could do those things to me, and how when I was 15, and everyone was moving out of our mother's home and he had offered me marijuana to let him do things to me, and when I was 17 and woke with him knelt beside where I was sleeping with his hand down the front of his underwear. So I said to him again, "I don't know who you think you're lying to?"

I then brought up the next subject that I wanted to confront him about, which was his daughter. I said to him, "While I have you on the phone, there's something else I'd like to discuss with you. A couple weeks after you disappeared, Jayson walked in on your seven-year-old daughter, having her 6 year old brother's penis in her mouth. When questioned about where she learned that, she said, "I like to have sex with my dad and ******. So that means you and your girlfriend were engaging in oral sex acts with your seven-year-old daughter?" "No wonder you disappeared in the middle of the night one night without a word to anyone," I said to him. He responded to what I had just said with the following, "What are you talking about, I haven't ever touched a child. I have four children here and you can ask my wife, my time to spend with my children is bath time, and she hasn't ever caught me doing anything to my children." As he said those words, I instantly had the same feeling that I was starting to notice would occur every time I thought of my oldest brother or even my cousins. My heart was racing, tears were burning my eyes, I felt extremely shaky, sick to my stomach, dizzy, and struck with an overwhelming feeling of anger and rage. "Did he honestly just say his time to spend with his kids is bath time?" I thought to myself. I again couldn't control the rage that I felt or the tears that ran down my cheeks. I screamed into the phone, "Why bath time *******?

Why?" And I disconnected the call. I couldn't believe what I had just heard. I was sick as I just lay in my bed in tears. I don't know why I had prayed that he had changed. Maybe it was because I hoped that he wasn't still hurting people. My heart went out to the nieces and nephews in Florida that I had never met, especially for the girls. And my heart hurt for all the others that he had hurt or violated over the years. I understood now that he would probably never change.

I should have never told Jayson how the phone call went, because it only intensified his hatred for our oldest brother. As I laid there that night lost in thought and unable to sleep, I was just so thankful that he never had nor ever would meet my children. At least for mine, I could see to it that they would never know what it was like to have their innocence robbed from them. To be honest, some people thought that it was extreme how I always checked the sex offender registry for my neighborhood at least once a week. And when I found out that there was a sex offender within the route that my daughter walked to middle school, I bought her a cell phone and pepper spray and showed her how to use the pepper spray. I then contacted the office at her school to find out what the protocol was for her carrying it with her to school, since it's considered a weapon. She had to check her keys in at the office when she got to school in the morning and then would pick them back up after her last class. I know this didn't ensure that nobody would hurt her, but it gave her awareness, she would always have a direct phone line home, and at least the pepper spray increased her defense.

Chapter 27

In 2009, my son was 9 and my daughter was 11, going on 12. Revisiting the memories of my oldest brother and my cousin reopened the wounds that I had long since put in a box and shoved as far back as I could on the top shelf of a closet, hoping that all the pain and memories would just go away. But they clearly had not. I was dealing with much more anxiety and depression and was having panic attacks a lot, sometimes while relaxing. My depression increased, and the constant fighting between my husband and me surely didn't help the situation. I just wanted him to find employment and help with the kids and the housework. I was so tired of coming home every day to a messy house and my kids in complete disarray while he was passed out in the living room.

I bottled up my thoughts and feelings a lot until I finally exploded. I was back to cutting myself on occasion. This had been a coping mechanism since I was young. Most times, my brain never seemed to shut down, and I tended to overanalyze everything. People often told me to stop cutting myself or asked why I cut myself. I guess for people who don’t suffer from mental illness, it’s hard to understand why people may self-mutilate. For me and my situation, at times when I was feeling sad or angry, my mind was like a movie reel on fast forward. When this happened, I didn’t know how to calm down because I didn’t know how to slow the thoughts. However, I had learned when I was younger and had started cutting myself that if I inflicted a little pain on myself, it would take a certain level of concentration away from the thoughts so that the mind would slow enough that I could start to calm down. Whenever I cut myself, it wasn't because I was trying to kill myself, or as people often accused, "doing it for attention." Rather, it was just a coping mechanism that I had used for years.

Suicidal thoughts and feelings of not being wanted or worthy of anything good, or feeling like everyone would be better off if I were dead, were almost daily thoughts that I had had since I was young. My self-esteem had never been good, and that was due to the fact that I was made fun of by my peers so much and I just felt like people were mean to me all the time. I had convinced myself that there was obviously something wrong with me that made people hate me. I have always been a little socially awkward. I was shy, quiet, timid, and often thought negatively. I hadn't ever experienced much positivity in my life.

It was around this time that I tried to start therapy because I couldn't seem to get out of the depressed slump that I was in. I had stayed so busy for years thinking that the memory of the horror that I had experienced for years would just go away if I didn't think about it. But my cousin's appearance the previous year had brought back nightmares that I thought I had escaped. Everyone kept telling me that I should go to therapy and be put on meds. So I tried. I was put on meds for depression and anxiety, and I started seeing a therapist. I poured out a lot about my past to my therapist, as well as the anxieties and depression I had been dealing with since the previous year. And I told her that I had to take a fan with me anywhere I would be sleeping, such as when we would go on a weekend vacation with the kids somewhere. If I couldn't focus on the sound of the fan's motor, I couldn't go to sleep, because I would hear every little noise possible in the middle of the night.

I didn't stay on meds for very long because I didn't like the way they left me feeling numb, foggy, and emotionless. Not to mention, having to prepare my mother's daily regimen of medicine every day as a child and growing up with an addict as a brother, I actually developed a phobia of taking pills. I didn't feel that telling the therapist about my past was making me feel any better either. I just felt exhausted every time I left her office. However, she said something to me one day that summed up a lot of how I had been feeling since the previous year. I was diagnosed with PTSD and panic attacks, on top of the depression and anxiety I had lived with for years. That brought a lot into perspective. But a couple of weeks later, I was told that my insurance wouldn't cover the therapist that I had been seeing for about a month. I felt annoyed and discouraged. It was a lot to tell someone about so much of my past that I didn't want to have to tell someone else everything I had already told this woman, so I just stopped going and instead just buried myself in my work and the kids again. At least if I didn't have any time to sit around, then I wouldn't have time to think about the past.

Beyond that, 2009 was just life as normal: work, home, and kids, oh yeah, and of course, fighting with my kids' dad all the time. He still wasn't working. When I would ask him to do something specific that needed to be done during the day while I was at work, such as the dishes, taking out the trash, or maybe vacuuming the floor, the tasks generally didn't get done. When I would say to him, "I thought you were going to do the dishes today?" he would always respond with, "I forgot." I had grown to hate the words "I forgot." How could anyone forget the one thing that they are supposed to do every single day? So, as if I actually had free time on my hands, I would have to do the dishes before I could cook dinner, or take the trash out before I could clean up the living room because it was already falling all over the floor from being so full. If I asked him to do laundry, every single time he would get one load in the dryer and the second load in the washer, and then he would forget again. I must say, one major pet peeve of mine is wrinkled clothes. So, now I would have to turn the dryer back on for a while to heat the clothes back up so I could fold them or hang them up while they were still warm to help prevent wrinkles. I was so irritated; he didn't want to work, he didn't want to help with the kids, and he didn't want to help lighten my load a little by helping with housework. It was always "I forgot," or "I'll do it in a minute," which would generally result in me doing whatever it was that I had asked him to do.

As 2009 faded into 2010, my 36th birthday was looming. I had feared being 36 since I was 14 years old, since that's the age that my mother was when she died. One of my biggest fears about becoming a mother was that I feared dying and leaving my children to grow up without a mother. I always felt cheated through life because I was just barely a teen when she passed. Thank goodness I had the love and support of Barb to help me through losing her. I always missed her, but this year was really going to be a lot harder for me. Depression hit me so hard at the beginning of 2010. Now when I wasn't at work, I was sleeping a lot. For people who have never dealt with depression, let me explain a little bit about what I was feeling on the inside and the thoughts I regularly had. Depression is wanting to be around people, but you're so depressed that you just want to be by yourself. Sometimes your mind races with all the negative stuff in life. It's wanting to get up and be productive, but your body physically hurts, and your mind is too exhausted to do anything. It's sometimes a feeling of hopelessness. And I steadily just continued to be more secluded from the outside world. Suicidal thoughts and thoughts of being insignificant and unloved haunted me constantly. I was cutting myself more. I guess I had feared that age and stressed about it for so long that it was almost as though I had a luminous cloud over me the moment I turned 36. I would force myself to take care of the kids and handle all the extracurricular stuff they had going on, but overall I was just going through the motions, feeling almost numb. I didn't have a choice other than to keep trudging through each day. Both kids were in the double digits for age now, which means my daughter was now 12, going on 13 in the fall, and my son was 10 at the beginning of 2010. Their dad and I at this point were kind of just coexisting. Over 18 years, I had grown much hatred towards the father of my children. When he would try to kiss me, I would turn my head and say, "Eew." There were a couple of instances that happened with the kids' father that were deciding factors for me that he and I could not remain together. A couple of days before Valentine's Day, when the four of us were in my van together, I stopped in front of Kmart and handed him a twenty-dollar bill, and I said to him, "Hey, will you take the kids in here and just let them pick me out something for Valentine's Day?" "I've taken care of the rest of the gifts, such as the ones to the kids from us, the one to you from the kids, and a gift to both of the kids from each other." "I'm not going into this store with these kids by myself," he responded back. So, I put the vehicle in drive and we went home. I could never understand why this man wouldn't do anything with his kids.

My children had been attending an after-school program next door to where we lived. My daughter had become interested in a boy who also attended the after-school program. I had started hearing the kid's name a lot. One day when there was no school, she asked me if she could go to Bever Park to meet up with one of her classmates and that girl's sister. I did question why they were at a park on the other side of town when we all lived on an opposite quadrant from where the park was. She responded, "I don't know, Mom, they're babysitting, and that's just where they are." I had an inkling that she really wasn't going to meet said friend at the park, so I decided to entertain the idea and told her to go get in the van.

When we arrived at the park, she said, "Okay, thank you, Mom, I'll see you later," as she went to get out of the van. "Whoa, wait a minute," I said to her. "Where are your friends?" "They're not here yet, they're on the way," she said to me. "Well, I know you don't think that I'm just going to drop you off by yourself in this big park. I'll wait with you," I said to her. She sighed and simply said, "Okay."

I heard her on the phone still, as she asked, "Where are you at?" And then she said to me, "They're coming from the pavilion over there, I'll see you later, Mom." "Just tell them to stay there and I'll drive you over there," I said to her. "No, just stay here," she said. She seemed a bit annoyed that I wouldn't just let her get out of the van and just leave her there. As we sat and continued to wait for her friends to come across the park from the pavilion, I could only see one person walking towards us from that direction. As the individual was halfway through the park, I could now clearly see exactly who it was. It was indeed the same little boy from the after-school program. Well, let's just say I definitely did not leave my daughter at the park that day. I was silent for the entire trip home because inside my mind I was thinking to myself, "just be fair, Rose. Think about where you were at her age and be fair." This only upset me more because when I was 12, I had multiple locks on the inside of my bedroom door trying to protect myself from my oldest brother and my father. I do know that none of that has anything to do with the situation with her.

I really just wanted her to understand the dangers of other possible outcomes had I just driven her to the park and dropped her off that day. From the young man that she went to meet with, and what his expectations of them meeting may have meant that day. And the other dangers that could have played a factor that day had I just dropped her off and driven away. I also explained to her that a relationship with someone can be a wonderful thing between two adults who love each other. I did take her cell phone away from her until the minutes ran out, and she had to wait a while before I let her have time on her phone again.

I did strive as hard as I could to discourage my kids from growing up too fast. I wanted them to enjoy their youth and just be a kid as long as they could. We have such a short window of time in our lives to be children. I never really got to be a child. Especially being a girl. I had to step up to the plate at a very young age and take care of my mom when she was sick, and clean and cook and I had to do housework and help make sure my brothers and I ate while my mom was in the hospital. And unless Jayson was around, I didn't really even get to play outdoors.

It was around this time that my family doctor referred me to a cardiothoracic surgeon due to the fact that on three separate occasions I had developed a blood clot in a superficial varicose vein on the inside of my right leg. Now these blood clots were not life-threatening because it wasn't a deep vein. It was more like it would cause an infection of sorts. It was painful and annoying more than anything. They did an ultrasound on both legs and told me that I had a bad vein in each leg and that the valve at the top had stopped working. So they scheduled me for two appointments that day. I would come back the first week, they would give me medicine to help me relax and numb the area that they would be running the catheter into. They would run the catheter up the vein and administer infrared heat to burn the vein closed as they backed the catheter back out of the vein. I was scheduled the following week to come back and have the left leg done.

When I walked into the office the following week, I wasn't feeling well. I was coughing a lot, my sinuses were backed up, and I was running a low-grade fever. They should not have proceeded with the procedure that day, but they did anyway. While backing the infrared heat out of the vein, they hit the inside of my left thigh and left a tiny surface burn. By the following day, I felt as if I couldn't breathe very well. I was coughing more, wheezing a lot, and my head was pounding. When I unwrapped my leg, I could see that where the tiny burn was, the whole inside of my left thigh was now super red and hot to the touch.

I decided to go to the emergency room, and my oxygen level was only in the upper 70's, which is fairly dangerous. So, I was admitted to the hospital with bronchitis, a sinus infection, and now cellulitis. With oxygen on and turned up all the way, I was still struggling to obtain 80% oxygen levels. I felt extremely weak and was struggling with each breath. To be honest, this was the only time that I had ever been hospitalized due to illness. They started three kinds of IV antibiotics, and I was receiving breathing treatments every two hours. I was also put on steroids and two inhalers.

The following morning, as I was sleeping while waiting to be taken down for a CT scan of my lungs, I was woken up when my husband came into my room. He hadn't come to see how I was doing because he was concerned about me. Instead, he came to see how I was doing because my presence was needed at home. Let me explain. He was literally in my hospital room yelling at me about what the kids were doing at home, and about the fact that he's not going to be at home alone with them until I got better and got out of the hospital. And that I would have to find someone else to babysit them if I thought I was just going to lay around in the hospital for days.

I still had no energy, and felt worse than I had ever felt in my life before, yet here was my husband, the father of my children, standing in my hospital room screaming at me. I was now not only super sick and completely weak, but also in tears.

Through tears, I just kept saying to him, "Please leave, please just leave." I didn't have the energy to fight with him or to be yelled at. A nurse that had been walking past my room with another patient had heard me crying and asking him to leave. So, after she got her other patient settled, she came into my room and asked if everything was okay. "I just wanted him to leave," I said to her. She then informed me that they would be taking me down to CT any time.

I then said to her, "When we come back up from CT, I have to go home." She said, "Rose, you're not going home today, you're not well enough to go home yet." As I began to cry again, I said to her, "That was my husband that you heard me in here with, he was up here screaming at me about what my children are doing at home. And he said that if I'm just gonna lay around up here, then I'll need to arrange for someone else to take care of the kids." "Rose, your doctor is not going to authorize you to be released today," she said to me. "You don't understand, my house doesn't run without me there, because he doesn't know how to take care of the children by himself." She told me to just try to relax and we'd talk about it after the CT scan was complete.

I was informed that day that I have COPD, and that my lungs were pretty sick due to the three infections in my body. I signed myself out of the hospital against doctor's orders and went home. I was sent home with four bottles of pills, two medicines for the nebulizer, and two inhalers. I was so sick that I wasn't even released to go back to work for about seven weeks. Yet I couldn't just lay in the hospital for a couple of days and get the IV antibiotics that would have helped speed up the recovery time a little. And why? Because the piece of shit man whose name I had taken and whom I had children with, couldn't step up to the plate for a couple of days. I knew by the time I was finally cleared to return to work that I was completely done with this worthless ass man. I just had to work out a plan as to how and when I would tell him that he needed to leave. If I was going to do it all by myself, then I may as well do it all by myself, without all the fighting and disrespect.

Shortly after I returned to work, I agreed to go to the third shift for the present season. I was going to work in a lead position. I had never worked a third shift position before, but

I thought that it would give me a little more time with my children. The plan was that I would sleep after work in the morning while the kids were at school.

In theory, it sounded good, but I quickly realized that I wasn't able to lay down when I would get home from work in the mornings because my son didn't start school until 8:50, and the kids' dad on multiple mornings wouldn't drive his son to school. Not that he was busy or had to go to work or anything, he just didn't want to. I mean, how hard is it for one to get into their vehicle and drive their child about 10 blocks away and drop them off? I hated how lazy and uninvolved he was in helping to handle the day-to-day responsibilities that come along with raising children. So most mornings I knew that I wouldn't be able to lay down until at least after 9:00 in the morning. Sometimes though, it would be later than that if the school had a late start due to weather. Some days it would be almost noon before I could lay down, and I'd just have to be back up before 3 to get the kids from school, and then I would have to cook dinner and spend time with the kids.

On many nights, I would go to work after only having an hour or two of sleep. Coffee and energy drinks became my best friends to make it through the shift. While working the night shift, I met a black gentleman, and he and I quickly became friends. With 2010 coming to an end also meant that I had almost completely made it through being the age of 36. It had been a really tough year battling depression, but I made it through it and I was still alive.

Chapter 28

Starting January 1, 2001, I paired with a friend from work for the biggest loser contest that our job was having. I was very serious about dieting this time. I eliminated a lot of carbs and sweets out of my diet and replaced them with lots of whole grains and fruit. I ate small amounts five times a day, drank 96 ounces of water every day, only ate lean meats such as turkey, chicken, and fish, and never ate after 6 pm. My children weren't the happiest with me at first, when I stopped buying a lot of the junk food for the house. They quickly learned that if they went to the store with me, the options on beverages did not consist of soda. And the only place that we went out to eat was Subway. By the end of January, I was down 36 pounds, and I was proud of myself. And I was now 37, so the fear of dying at the age of 36 was behind me. It's almost as if the luminous cloud had finally dissipated.

My children's father finally obtained employment probably three weeks into January. He was working at Goodwill going through donation bins. However, by this point, I was finished with trying to get this individual to just be a dad. I shouldn't have to keep begging him to be involved with his children, and what was between us at one point, had been gone for the past ten years. I had started planning for the day that I was going to tell him to leave. I had become distant and quiet with him. I had so much hatred for this man, the sheer sound of his voice made my blood pressure rise.

On Valentine's Day, he came home with a dozen roses for me. This man had never bought me flowers in 18 years, why now? Maybe because of the distance I had put between us. Now all of a sudden he wanted to converse with me, but it was too late. On Friday, February 18, 2011, I told my husband that we were finished. I had opened a new bank account and taken my name off our joint account. At that time, we had about $3,500 in our account due to tax money. I left $1,500 in the joint account for him and transferred the other $2,000 into my new account, because the children would be staying with me. I figured that would be enough for him to get established somewhere.

On Friday, I picked the kids up from school and I had prearranged for them both to go stay the weekend with family, as I was working overtime at work all weekend. And I didn't think that the children needed to be present when I told their father that he needed to move out. I was in the kitchen scrambling hamburgers for the taco bar we were having at work that night when he came home from work. He came into the kitchen and was in an unreasonably good mood just talking away. He said to me, "A couple of my buddies and I were joking around the other day about, wouldn't it be funny if we were to find a dildo or something in one of the donation bins. Lo and behold, look what I found today," he said as he pulled a vibrator out of his pocket. I looked at him and said, "What are you going to do with that?" "I brought it home for you," he replied. "You brought me home a used dildo?" I asked him. "I washed it," he said back to me. I said, "Again, you brought me home a used dildo?" "The fact that you even picked that up with your hands makes me sick to my stomach." "That could have been up a dog's ass for all I know," I said to him. "I won't be using that. You can throw it in the garbage unless you need it for something," I said to him. It just made what I had to say to him even easier. I seriously couldn't believe this man. Nothing says I love you after 18 years like a used dildo.

"Actually, there's something I want to talk to you about," I said to him. So began the conversation about me ending our marriage. I had begged this man for 13 years just to be a father. I hadn't been in love with him for 10 years. I was so tired of fighting and being depressed and disrespected. I told him that I left him $1500 in our joint account and that I had taken my name off that account. He said things like "Please just give me another chance, I promise I'll change." "What could you possibly show me that you haven't shown me in 18 years?" I asked him. "How many chances do you think you get?" "I can't do this with you anymore." "I haven't been in love with you for 10 years, and I'm so tired of you not helping with the kids, the house, or the bills," I said to him. "I have a job now, Rose," he said. "Well, it's about time; you haven't contributed in years." "I'm sorry, I've made up my mind, I honestly can't do this with you anymore," I said. "I know you've been feeling the distance. Why do you think you bought me roses for Valentine's Day this year?" "We've been together for 18 years and you've never bought me anything." I told him that the kids were with family for the weekend, and that I had rented a room for the weekend, so he could have a couple of days to get his stuff together. I told him that Jayson said that he could stay with him for a little while until he figured out what his next move was going to be. I told him that if he decided that he wasn't going to leave, that I would pack mine and the children's things, and we would move out. It was obvious that neither one of us was happy, because otherwise we wouldn't fight constantly, and all the toxicity wasn't healthy for anyone involved. I told him that he was welcome to call or see the kids whenever he wanted to, and that I would never stop him from seeing them unless he put them in danger. And I told him that as long as he helped me with the kids' needs, that I wouldn't file for child support. I carried the roaster of meat that I had made for work out to my van, and then went back inside to grab the bag of clothes and hygiene items that I had packed for the weekend. "I'll call you Sunday morning when I get off work and you can let me know what you've decided," I said to him. And then I left and went to the hotel to sleep for a couple of hours until I had to be at work.

I called him on Sunday morning and asked him what he had decided, and he said, “I’m not fucking going anywhere, Rose.” I calmly responded, “Okay then, I will be there in just a little while to start packing mine and the kids’ things.” “Whatever, I’ll fucking leave,” he screamed back at me. I told him that I would give him until the evening to get his stuff together. Later that night, I picked the children up and we went home. And I sat and had a conversation with the kids about my decision and why I had made that decision. I told them that I had stayed with their father unhappily for too long and it was about time that I was fair to myself, not to mention how toxic the environment had been for many years. The kids quickly adjusted to the new routine. And for a while, they would sometimes try to call their dad and not get an answer, so they would wait for him to call, and still not hear from him. I do recall one time when I called and asked him, “Do you realize you haven’t called your children in over a month?” He responded with, “Well, they know my number.” “You’re right, but they got tired of you not answering, so they decided just to wait for you to call them. That was a month ago, besides, aren't you a parent?” I asked him.

At first, I had to argue with him sometimes to let the kids come see him. He was always too tired or busy and didn't really want to be bothered with his kids. Sometimes when the children were visiting him, he would still call my phone screaming at me, "Rose, you better get your fucking son." I hated the fact that I couldn't ever just get an hour to myself, because he couldn't handle his kids. In fact, very early on in the breakup, I often had to send the kids with food in order for them to be able to eat while they were there. Probably a couple of weeks after I made him move out, the new friend that I had met at work came over one day while the kids were at school. There was a mutual attraction between the two of us. While he and I were hanging out that day, he told me that the older female that I often saw him leave work with sometimes was indeed his woman. He told me that she was 12 years older than him, and that they had been together for 11 years, and that he had no intentions of leaving her. He told me that he just liked to spend time with and entertain women. He told me that he would never be with me and me alone, that that's just who he is. He told me if it got to a point that I couldn't handle it anymore that we would part ways. I know in a nutshell, the scenario sounds kind of messed up, but I was very attracted to this man, and I had just gotten out of an 18-year relationship, and didn't want a full-time relationship at that time anyway. As a matter of fact, we had no intention of my children meeting him. However, as April came about, my breasts started hurting like they had only hurt two other times in my life, which would have been the pregnancy of my two children. My friend told me to buy a pregnancy test, and I said to her, "Girl, I can't get pregnant, I was cut, tied, and burnt." However, with my breasts continuing to hurt, on April 15th, I finally went and bought one. Much to my surprise, the test was positive. I sat in shock for a while. Then came the thought, "Oh my god, how am I going to tell this man that I'm pregnant? Especially when I told him that I can't get pregnant."

When I spoke with him on the phone, he was just as confused and shocked as I was. Then came the question, "So what are you going to do?" "Well, I don't believe in abortion," I responded. "Well, I guess we'll deal with it then." By the next day, it was starting to sink in a little more, and so I decided to tell the kids. This also meant that now that they knew, I kind of had to put a face with the name eventually. It was inevitable that if I was going to have this man's child, my kids were going to have to meet him.

However, 4 days after taking the pregnancy test, I started bleeding quite a bit and was having really bad lower abdominal pain. I went to the emergency room to be seen. They performed an internal ultrasound, and after the results were read by a doctor, I was taken straight to the operating room. I had an ectopic pregnancy. The fetus had started growing in my right fallopian tube, so I had to have emergency surgery to have my right tube removed and the pregnancy terminated. I was kind of sad, but at the same time relieved. I never did want children with multiple men, and to be honest, I didn't really want to start all over again, considering my son was now 11. Sometimes in life, things happen for a reason, and in this case, it was probably for the best. Especially considering his situation.

I did always enjoy the time that my friend and I spent together. He always encouraged me through the weight loss that I was going through that year, and he always said things to uplift me and make me feel good about myself. Most of the time, we would just sit and listen to music and talk for hours.

A couple of months after the ectopic pregnancy was terminated, we were hanging out in my computer room listening to music and talking. He was sitting in the computer chair, and I was standing by the desk. I had an incense burning as I often had. All of a sudden, the incense became overpowering, so I grabbed it and snuffed it out. As soon as I put it out, my stomach tightened up, and I had three really quick spins. The next thing I knew, I woke up on the floor with my friend asking me if I was okay. I hadn't completely finished with the seizure, but I knew I needed to get to the restroom asap, I needed to empty my stomach before I had a mess. My body was still convulsing a little. I ended up knocking the toilet paper holder off the bathroom wall trying to get to the bathroom in time. As soon as I emptied my stomach, the spins dissipated.

I hadn't had a seizure in 19 years and this one actually took a lot out of me. I have to admit, it was kind of scary after 19 years of not having one. I thought that I had grown out of my seizure disorder. I did contact my family physician and was scheduled for an appointment with neurology as well as for an EEG. Now for those that don't know what an EEG is, it's where they attach what seems like 100 wires to your head, and they have you lay still and completely relax, and as you fall asleep, they monitor your brain activity. Since strobe lights and such are known to trigger seizures, they also do a series of strobes and such while they're monitoring the brain's responses. The neurologist did restart me on anti-seizure medication and I was informed that my license was suspended for 6 months, but if I had another seizure before the next six months were over, I would have my license suspended for longer.

I quickly remembered why I didn't like taking the anti-seizure meds when I was younger. They always made me feel fuzzy and a little disoriented. I had always felt, due to my epilepsy, as though my equilibrium and balance had been off. And the fuzzy kind of aura from the medicine surely didn't make that any better. I stopped taking the medicine about two weeks later. Now if I were to start having seizures on a regular basis, I would take the meds, but I didn't feel that one seizure after 19 years warranted taking a pill every day for the rest of my life nor having to deal with the fuzzy feeling.

Besides, I had a bit of a phobia when it came to taking pills. I'm sure that was due to the fact that I used to get my mother's meds ready for the day every morning. And the side effects of meds really bothered me too. I felt that the world of taking pills was a very vicious cycle. Half the time one can be prescribed one medication for something, and end up taking two more as a result of the side effects caused by the first medication. I could say that I have had to go through panic attacks all day just to start taking a new medication.

After six months, I was able to renew my driver's license, but was informed that I could only renew for two years and would have to see the neurologist and have him fill out a paper for the Department of Transportation before I could renew in two years. My friend and I were still hanging out quite a bit. In fact, on multiple occasions, he would stay over for a couple of days here, and a week there. I was starting to fall in love with this man, but I always had to remember that we were just friends. He was always very supportive and always said things that were uplifting and made me feel better about myself as I continued my weight loss journey.

However, I do remember one time that I snapped at him. I had gone into my daughter's room one day to talk to her about something, and when I was in there, she was telling me that there was a school dance that Friday and asked if I would give her money to go. As she asked me, I happened to see bills sticking up out of her bank. So I said to her, "You have money in your bank, why don't you use that for the dance?" "As a matter of fact, where did you get that from?" I asked her. I was kind of shocked at her response. "I can't tell you," she said. "Excuse me, what do you mean you can't tell me?" I asked her. So I asked her again, "Where did you get that money from?" She told me that she wasn't supposed to tell me that my friend would give her like $5-$10 once in a while when he would come over. I reiterated to my daughter, "You don't ever keep secrets from me," I told her. "As a matter of fact, nobody should ever tell you not to tell me something. If anyone ever tells you again not to tell me something, I want you to come directly to me." "Do you understand me?" I asked her. She nodded in response. "I mean it, don't ever let a grown person tell you not to tell me something or that it's you and their secret." I almost felt panicked that if she would keep a smaller secret, what other kind of secret would she keep?

Later when I spoke with my friend, I asked him why he had been giving my daughter money, and even more, why did he ask her not to tell me. He said that he had been giving her $5 or so at a time because he wanted to teach her how to save money, and he told her that when she had $100 saved up, then she could open a savings account with it. I was still extremely annoyed with the whole situation, and I told him that I didn't want him giving my daughter money anymore, and furthermore not to ever tell my daughter to not tell me something. I told him that we don't do secrets in my house. He was kind of hurt for me getting on him at first because he thought giving her money was something innocent, but in my eyes, if an adult has to say to a child, "Don't tell your mom," then they shouldn't be doing what they're doing.

Chapter 29

By the following January, which was one year after I started the weight loss contest at work, I had lost 127.4 lbs. I truly hadn't been that light since the age of 10 when I had started my menstrual cycle and developed. I loved that I could go to the smaller section when shopping for clothes. And it felt really good to actually have a size. I was really proud of myself. I felt really good in all the new cute little outfits that I wore. I still felt fat and hated the way that I looked when I would get undressed because now I had all this excess skin hanging off of me. I met with a plastic surgeon to see about getting a tummy tuck to get rid of some of the excess skin, but even though I paid a nice amount for some good health insurance, they wouldn't cover the surgery.

When I received my taxes the following year, I decided to move out of the house that I had been renting for 4 years. I decided that an apartment would be easier because I wouldn't have to worry about lawn care or pay all of the utilities like I did with the rental house.

When we moved into the apartment, things were going pretty well. The children and I quickly adjusted to apartment life as well as to our schedules. I was still maintaining my new weight and healthier lifestyle. My friend and I were still hanging out, but things were quickly becoming more complicated. I truly had fallen in love with this man, so the time we spent apart was now strained with jealousy, sadness, and loneliness. In fact, it had come to the point that I just couldn't do it anymore. I loved him, but couldn't deal with the mental anguish and overwhelming depressed feeling that I was feeling regularly. I shut down all communication with him so that I could heal my broken heart. I had indeed learned about myself over the year and a half that he and I had spent together, that I wasn't capable of spending that much time with an individual and not allowing feelings to develop.

So I created a profile on a dating website, as I was open to meeting new people. Almost all of the people that I messaged never even got to the point where we met face to face. And if I did agree to meet anyone, I always made sure that it was in a very public meeting place.

Alongside that, however, I just buried myself with working overtime at work to help keep my mind occupied until I was over being love sick. It would be safe to say that I was very good at staying as busy as I could to occupy my mind, so I didn't overthink stuff a lot. I overthought everything. Whenever someone said something to me, my brain would replay what I just heard and then instantly start picking it apart. Or like if someone didn't answer their phone, or called me back about something, my mind would already make up about 20 different scenarios about what was going on, and of course most of them were negative. The reason I overthought everything was because as a child, I never really had anyone to talk to about things, especially when Jayson would be gone in lockup somewhere, so I had to just think through everything on my own. In fact, sometimes when I had a lot on my mind, I would seclude and isolate myself away from the rest of the world until I worked through all the thoughts in my head. I felt like I had a movie reel playing in my head constantly.

It's probably safe to say that I was drinking quite a bit in those days. It had pretty much become a nightly thing, so that when I went to bed at night, I wouldn't have to lie awake for hours lost in thought. Or so I didn't lie in the dark and think about how lonely I was all the time. All I had ever wanted in my life was to be with one man who was just as crazy in love with me as I was with him. Someone I could go to bed with and wake up with. Someone I could be at my best with, but who could love me at my worst. I always hated going to bed at night by myself, often with so much to talk about but nobody to talk to. I'd have to say, at the end of the day, as I lay alone in my bed, that's when I always felt the loneliest. So if I drank every night, I wouldn't have to feel all these emotions or have all these thoughts. I would just pass out. It seemed easier for a while. However, the drinking only lasted for about a couple of months, before I was back to feeling better about the broken heart. Before long, I was chatting with people online and had created a profile on a couple of dating websites.

I was just trying to meet new people. In a blink of an eye, 2012 was quickly approaching the end. Fall was now just ahead on the horizon. This was the time of year where people started trading in their shorts and flip-flops for hoodies and bonfires. With Labor Day approaching quickly, people were enjoying the impending end of the warm summer-like days. And as with every Labor Day, efforts were well underway for raising and collecting money for the MDA. One afternoon, I had to run to the gas station just down the hill from our apartment. As I started coming down the hill, I could see that a local group of firefighters was at the intersection collecting donations in their boots. So, as I stopped at the stop sign at the bottom of the hill, I told one of the firefighters to give me just a minute to run into the store, and after I got change, I would stop and put some money in his boot. Just as I promised, I stopped after leaving the station. I dropped $7 and some change, and in exchange, he handed me a sticker and thanked me as I also thanked him. As I began my incline back up the hill, I looked at the sticker that he had handed me. It read, "I donated to the MDA." Instantly I burst into tears. By the time I made it to the drive of the apartments, I was sobbing uncontrollably. Why? Because I knew how much our parents had stolen from that organization over a five-year period. Sadly, they used us three kids to collect the money for them. And we children knew better than to say anything about what they had done because discipline was always fairly harsh. I hated that they had used us children to steal all the time. I hated that all that money didn't make it to the MDA.

After I arrived home from the station, I lay in my bed just lost in thought. I thought about how wrong my parents had been in the MDA situation. And as my mind wandered, I thought about my entire childhood all the way back to the earliest of my memories, which would have been the age of three in Ft. Madison in that apartment above the store, when I was so vibrant and full of life, and unknowing of the horrid life I would face over the upcoming years. I never have forgotten the love that I had for my cat here, Sam. I pray he had a good life and shared the love with his new family that he showed to me. Jayson pushing me out of the car at that age was something that I have never forgotten. Then onto the next house still unsuspecting of the future terrors that were lurking around the corner. Here, the horror of the night that the individual was pounding on the doors and windows as my mother and I worked on laundry. How scary it was that night when Jayson and I were sent across the street in the middle of the night to wake the neighbor to call my dad and the police. That had to be among the most terrifying memories from my youngest years. Of all three children, why was it always the two youngest ones she sent to do all the scary stuff, while her pride and joy she kept with her? And yes, it was well known in our house that he was her favorite because he was her firstborn. Both of us were terrified that night. As we stepped down from the doorstep, I don't even think my feet hit pavement, as we held hands Jayson ran as fast as he could, and with me being significantly shorter, I did feel like I glided that night. We both stood there terrified, shaking, waiting for the neighbor to wake from us pounding on the door. And what was probably only 60 seconds seemed like an eternity to the two of us. The experience from that night would be something we all would never forget. Besides my other big memory from this house, which just so happened to be, the milk drinking contest between Jayson and myself. I am currently 49 years old and I can honestly say that I have never allowed anyone to pour me a glass of milk since that day. I literally have to be able to open the jug and smell it, or I won't even drink milk.

As I continued to look and reflect back on my life from my earliest memory to the current, I thought about when my oldest brother started his middle of the night visits to my room. I thought about why my mom always told me that I couldn't talk about what my brother was doing to me, "Because these bad people will take us away and we'll never see each other again." Or my parents constantly telling me that I couldn't go outside without Jayson because "Bad things happen to little girls outside." Those two statements were ones that were heard often in my home. Why weren't measures put in place to ensure my safety from my oldest brother? Why wasn't he ever disciplined for his actions? Why was it acceptable and allowed to continue going on? I actually recall one time while living in this trailer that my father had caught my brother Jayson touching himself in his genital area, and my dad had beaten the shit out of Jayson. Yet the oldest brother was allowed to keep molesting me without ever being disciplined. None of it made sense. Still, at the age of 49, I didn't know the answers to any of those questions.

Next up on reflecting, starting kindergarten and the beginning of the taunting that started happening almost immediately once I started school. It really bothered me right from the beginning. I didn't understand why these kids were so mean to me. It wasn't my fault that I wore the clothes that I wore, those were the only clothes I had. Like most children, we didn't exactly get to go to a department store and go shopping with our mom, we didn't get new outfits from our parents or friends and family for our birthdays or Christmas.

There weren't those things, because there was never money for new things. Whenever my parents did have a little money, which was generally because us children had made it for them, you know from having to constantly pick up and collect for them. To the point that we were made to climb in garbage cans or dumpsters (something else for my peers to torment me about, cause now I'm a garbage digger) or even made to steal cans and bottles from people's yards, porches, and garages. That money generally went to buying cigarettes and drinks for them. Sometimes they would even have us kids walking the ditch alongside the highway to look for cans for them, and they would literally have us keep walking the ditch and picking up cans and bottles, while they rode ahead to the next town to buy themselves a soda, and sometimes a treat, which was usually milk duds for my mother and a 3 musketeer candy bar for my father.

It was nice when I could go follow Jayson around, because we explored a lot and did fun adventurous things, you know, like kids are supposed to do. There was sometimes that Jayson probably didn't have my best interest in mind, like when he'd have some clever idea in mind to try to talk me into something knowing I would fall or hurt myself. He got tired of feeling like I was tattling on him, when I wasn't intentionally trying to get him beat with the paddle made out of a one by four, with holes drilled in it that read "****** and ******* board for the kids' asses," rather my mother would tell me to watch my brothers and I was told that I needed to tell her if they were getting into trouble. Now looking at that time frame of my life, I can actually say, I never really got to be a kid.

At this age, I had to learn how to cook simple things like scrambled eggs, toast, soup, sandwiches, hot dogs, mac & cheese, etc.....

Whenever my mom was in the hospital, I had to ensure that her husband and boys were fed, make sure her house stayed clean to her standards, and I had to look after my brothers to make sure they weren't getting into any trouble. The craziest part of all this was that I was the youngest member of the family. It sure seemed like a lot of responsibility for such a little girl. I was barely 6 and had already grown beyond my years. And whenever my mom wasn't in the hospital, I was taking care of her.

As my mind continued to wander through my memories of my childhood, I thought about my 7th birthday. We didn't expect presents or cake and ice cream for birthdays, but we would at least get acknowledged by the other members of the house and be told Happy Birthday. My feelings were so hurt on this day; it seemed like everyone had seriously forgotten my birthday that year. I remember being really sad that day. Then I had to go to school and endure the same usual kids who tormented me making fun of me for something and tormenting me some more. We'll get to my feelings about the tormenting by my peers, but for now, back to the birthday. By the time I climbed onto the school bus to go home, I remember feeling tired and just super sad. As I came in the door to our trailer, my dad, paddle in hand, and yes it's true, I really did receive the wrath of my father's enjoyment that year, was in tears by the second swing. I remember with each swing, he laughed and carried on and swung even harder each time. That birthday spanking was definitely something I had carried for many years.

The next memory around this time would be becoming immune to the people laughing at us and calling us names like scrounge, garbage diggers, welfare babies, "Ha ha your parents are poor," "Rose is wearing her grandma's shoes, look they have holes in them," "Ha ha this, ha ha that," even screaming it at us as a car drove by. We were basically put on public display for everyone to laugh at and ridicule. The torment from my peers, I will be honest, caused me immeasurable amounts of my own self-hatred. I began to think around that time that there really must be something wrong with me to make everyone be mean to me and to cause them to not like me. I would mentally tear myself up with thoughts of feeling ugly and fat and gross and disgusting because that's what everyone was saying to me. At this point, mind you, the torment at school was going on, while in my home life, I was sick of my brother doing that nasty stuff to me. I remember laying stiff as a board on multiple nights in an attempt to hopefully make my oldest brother get tired of fighting with my clothes and go back to bed. His visits, however, were still persistent. And most times I couldn't fight and stay stiff enough for him to not at least get my bottoms off. Why did I have to keep this horrible secret for the rest of them? Well, except for Jayson, of course. I actually missed him more than anything whenever he would be locked up again from place to place.

It was also around this time that the school asked my mom if they could move me from 2nd grade to 4th grade. My mother was not supportive of this and did not allow me to have my mind stimulated with my education. The work that we were doing in second grade didn't challenge me. This bothered me a lot, and I'd never forget it. My daughter had been in advanced placement classes since middle school. She was reading college-level books at the age of 10. I remembered having to sign consent for her to take AP classes. I always encouraged my daughter to live to her fullest potential. I encouraged recognition of awards and such that she would get. I wanted her to live to be the best "amazing" that she was capable of.

As my memories continued, I remember the campgrounds when we were homeless. Pollmiller Park in West Point, Iowa. I remember us kids all day every day were sent out to keep scouring the park for cans and bottles as well as people's belongings. I remembered that since Jayson was really fast and good at retrieving wallets out of people's jeans or purses that were left with their towels and other items on the beach as they cooled off in the water. It was sickening how much our parents used us kids to make up for their shortcomings as members of society as well as parents.

From the campgrounds, we moved to a farmhouse. Here, the landlord had agreed to allow my father to pay rent or part of the rent by feeding his cattle and chickens each day. However, it seemed no matter what type of work my father attained, it wouldn't be long before he quit. So yet again, rent wouldn’t be covered, and we would have to move.

It was ridiculous that he couldn't even continue something as simple as feeding the animals every day to keep a roof over his family's heads.

After the farmhouse, we moved to Faith’s Apple Orchard farmhouse. I remember all the long walks to West Point, 10 miles each way. We had to pick up cans all day, every day, as our parents worked for the carnival. I remembered dodging bats as we walked the 10 miles back home in the middle of the night, carrying bags of cans for our parents. Jayson and I used to have fun feeding the horses apples here. The horses loved the apples, and we thought it was fun watching them slobber all over themselves. Jayson also caught timber rattlers, a humongous toad, and stick spiders.

I also remembered breaking my collarbone there and the awful brace I had to wear as a result. I wasn't sure how someone's collarbone could break by simply extending an arm forward. Didn't the doctor find that a little strange? I could honestly say it was not normal for one's bones to break that easily. However, we weren’t allowed to drink milk because my father would throw a fit if he didn’t have milk to make a glass of crackers and milk. Disgusting. Besides, a parent should always ensure their child is fed before themselves, as well as make sure their children are getting the vital vitamins and nutrients they need to grow. The only milk I ever got was the one little carton with my lunch at school. Children could also have a carton of milk each afternoon, provided there was money in their milk account. Well, as you can imagine, there definitely wasn't any money on any accounts for us children because the extra money my parents ever had, above rent, was for cigarettes and soda.

I also remembered from this place the day Jayson thought it was a clever idea to piss off a bull and make it chase him. Let's just say, I don't think he had calculated that the bull would be able to move that fast. Nor did he clear the barbed wire fence; instead, he ended up coming through it. Most importantly, Jayson learned a valuable lesson that day, and I don't think he would ever make the decision again to piss off a bull and then try to outrun it.

Chapter 30

As I continued looking back on my life, I remembered next moving to the yellow house on the double hill. I always helped my mom with laundry and housework. She used to make me stay home from school sometimes because she didn't want to be alone. Sometimes, when she kept me home from school, I would cry. I still got bullied on a daily basis, but whenever Jayson was in placement, school was my only way to get out of the house for a while. You know, because "bad things happen to little girls outside." I was so sick of hearing my parents make that statement.

Especially since I now knew that what they meant is that little girls could get raped or abducted. But wait a minute, hadn't I been getting sexually assaulted in my home for 5 years? So maybe they were only referring to strangers sexually assaulting me, since they knew what my brother had been doing to me for years. And of course 4 of my cousins as well.

This would be the home that we lived in when I started my menstrual cycle and would begin the daily ritual of punching myself in the stomach as hard as I could over and over. This was also where we lived when the harshness of the punishments that we endured became more apparent. From our oldest brother having to wear urine-saturated underwear on his head with the crotch on his nose, to getting our fingertips burned, to having to chew on a chunk of bar soap, and having to swallow it. I think I would have much-preferred dish soap over bar soap.

I remember being super frustrated around this time. While it was nice to finally celebrate Christmas in 1984, I was tired of never being able to just go play outside with the neighborhood kids. I hated when it rained and we were made to go catch night crawlers at the park. I was sick of having to eat the nasty fish my parents caught in the Mississippi. I was tired of having to steal for our parents. I was tired of being made fun of due to my parents making us collect cans and bottles for them all the time. I was so tired of my oldest brother's middle-of-the-night visits. By that stage, I lay awake most nights in complete darkness with my ears peaked. Listening for a squeak of the floor, or the rustle of clothing, or the creek of the door, so that I could mentally prepare myself that my brother was coming into my room again.

I always loved when Jayson was home from placement, well besides when he was being mean to me. Like every time he and the social worker were around each other. The beating I took with the flyswatter that one day as a result of our social worker, was something that stayed with me my entire life. There was a good possibility that she had passed away, because she was extremely unhealthy all those years ago when she was our worker.

However, if she had still been alive, and I had happened to see her, this is exactly what I would have said to her: "Really, employed by the state of Iowa to protect children? Bitch, you made me sick to my stomach." And I would have spit right in that bitch's face. I didn't hold this against Jayson, because just like myself, we were still children. The worker, though, was a grown woman and a social worker at that. I'm sure that the Department of Human Services would not have been okay with her actions. It just made me wonder how many other children were harmed under her care.

I also recalled one time when we came home from getting groceries and I was trying to carry the watermelon up to the house, but the step from the road to the first step at the bottom still had a cinder block as a step in the road today because Jayson and my father were the only two who could get up that really tall step due to their long legs. Well, as I tried to maneuver the steps, I accidentally dropped the watermelon, for which I took a beating. I began spending a lot of time in my room when we lived in this house because I didn't have any friends that I was allowed to go outside and play with, and I got tired of always being with my parents. I don't think any child wants to be around their parents all the time. I wrote a lot back then because I was never really allowed to have a voice. So my communication skills weren't the best. I would write down the things that I wanted to say to people, but that I would either get in trouble for or didn't have the confidence to say. Communicating to people how they made me feel when they made me feel that way is something I had spent a lot of time working on recently because I would bottle everything up and hold it in until I became an explosive emotional mess. I found a lot of solace in listening to music.

I remember my mother had become very sick while we lived here also. I mean she had always been sick a lot, but her doctor had ordered an allergy test that instantly sent her into anaphylactic shock. They tested her for 70 things, and 56 of them flared up. She was so sick that we had a hospital bed, wheelchair, and oxygen in the home for a while. Not only was she allergic to 56 things out of 70, but she also had really bad Asthma and heart disease. When she was 13, she had rheumatic fever and it damaged the lower half of her right lung, so they had indeed done surgery and took out the lower half of that lung. And mind you that she was at least a 2 pack a day cigarette smoker. I was my mother's caregiver from the age of like 4-5. She took over 100 pills a day and I knew what she needed, at what times, and what they were all for. Along with the different inhalers she had, and the attachment that had to be put on certain ones. I didn't mind taking care of my mom, cause that's what I had always done. I just really wanted to be outdoors laughing and running around carefree like all the other kids in the neighborhood were.

I remembered when my mom cut my hair off where it was basically a boy's haircut, because I didn't brush my hair after my bath the night before. It would hurt to have my hair brushed, and I hated it when she would brush my hair, because if I moved at all or winced, she would crack me in the head with the hairbrush and tell me to sit still. But honestly, like I wasn't tormented enough by my peers, she gave me a boy's haircut so they could make fun of me more. I remember being so socially awkward that I would ask kids who were nice to me, "Do you like me?" "Are you my friend?" Jayson used to laugh at me when I said things like that, but in fact, I was always jealous of Jayson, because he had a lot of friends. I hate looking back at my school pictures. some of the awful outfits that I was dressed in for picture day, no wonder my peers made fun of me. Besides the fact that I was shy, timid, lacked self-esteem, and lacked social skills.

In early 1985, we moved into what would be the last residence we lived in in Ft. Madison. There, I remember the powwow my father had with me when he caught me smoking. I can't say that even today I understand the concept behind making us smoke a bunch of cigarettes in hopes that we would get sick and wouldn't want to smoke any more. Let me just say, all of us kids were addicted to nicotine before we were even born.

And to grow up in a home where roughly 5 packs of cigarettes a day were smoked around us, in the house, and even in the car with the windows rolled up frequently. So how was increasing the nicotine in our system going to fix the addiction to nicotine? Extremely silly if you ask me.

I also, while looking back, thought of when our oldest brother had sex with a much older woman in my parent's bed and the bloody mess that was left behind. My mother knew it wasn't from her, but I couldn't say that I recalled him being disciplined for the situation. In fact, our mother babied and protected our oldest brother quite a bit. It appeared he never faced any discipline for any of the sexual incidents. Why was that? Of all the things that we always got in trouble for, I never recalled him getting in trouble for violating me. I often wondered where my oldest brother had learned the things that he did to me on a regular basis in the middle of the night. He might have learned it from some of our older male cousins. Or had it possibly been deeper than that? For a while, I thought that was what older male cousins and such did to the girls. I believed that the weird sexual stuff between siblings and cousins hadn't just occurred in our house, but in all of our cousins' homes as well.

The next of my reflections on my life, brought me back to my cousin coming to stay for a couple of days fresh out of the army. I recalled the first day he had arrived, and when I found him and the boys in the basement smoking marijuana. I recalled smoking weed for the first time that day. I remembered having a major case of the giggles and feeling extremely hungry after smoking. I liked the way it made me feel. I didn't feel as sad and withdrawn when I was high, rather more relaxed and carefree. I believe we smoked 2-3 times that day.

That night our cousin was sent upstairs to sleep where the boys' room was. In the middle of the night that night, I felt the all too familiar moving of my blanket and then my panties, I tried to reach for my panties to pull them back up. I was tired and just wanted my oldest brother to leave me alone.

All of a sudden, I felt this huge hand cupping my mouth and nose. I couldn't move, there was someone really heavy on top of me. And then I felt this big thrust that hurt so bad that I let out a scream. Or I tried to at least. It's kind of hard to scream though when you have a huge hand covering most of your face. I could hear him breathing and kinda moaning with each thrust. And in between the moans and grunts, he said to me, "Shhhh…." "You better not tell anybody about this, do you hear me?" "If you tell anyone you will regret it, 'cause I will hurt you, do you understand?" I tried to nod in agreement, but I couldn't move my head much with the force of his hand on my face. Finally, he let out one last groan before he climbed off of me and said, "Remember what I said." He then retreated back upstairs. I laid there in pain crying thinking about his threats.

Sadly enough, who would I have told? My mom had been telling me for years that we couldn't talk about it, cause the state would take us away and we'd never see each other again.

The following day, he made his presence known and would mumble threats to me whenever we crossed paths. Just as quickly as he arrived at our house, he was gone. The next thing I remembered from this house was finding Jayson in the basement completely out of it. He had been huffing gas fumes out of a gas can. Not sure where he had learned how to do something like that, but my mother and Aunt LuAnn hogtied him and drove him to Cromwell in Independence, Iowa for drug treatment.

It wasn't too long after that, that my parents went to the Old Threshers and Settlers reunion with my aunt and uncle. Not sure why my mother would have even considered going there with all her health conditions. By the following day, they still hadn't returned from this outing. Instead, my father and another aunt arrived saying that our mother was in the hospital, and that we needed to get some clothes together as we would be staying at my aunt's for a while.

Within a couple of days, it was said that our mother's condition had worsened and she was considered to be on her "death bed." I know that another aunt had flown in from Seattle as our mother was not expected to live much longer. Crazy enough, I know for certain that while our mother was expected to die, my father was sleeping with her sister when her husband was at work. As a matter of fact, this aunt later in life asked Jayson if he would engage in a threesome with her and another of our mother's sister's husband. Now if that doesn't put into perspective how messed up our entire family on my mother's side was, then I don't know what will. By whatever small miracle, our mother pulled through and began her road to recovery. I remember living in an upstairs duplex apartment for what must have only been a month or so. To be honest, it couldn't have been long, because I don't even remember the layout of this apartment.

From there we moved across the street from a local dairy factory. I remembered being so excited about having locks on my bedroom door. If nobody else was gonna stop my oldest brother from the middle of the night visits, at least I could protect myself. It felt so good to lock them the first time. It was extremely liberating. Life was way better for me than it had ever been. I recall several nights he would knock on my door and whisper through it for me to unlock my door. I would just lay in my bed and act like I didn't hear him.

Then came the night that my father asked me to sleep with him. I truly was Daddy's girl up to this point. Looking back on that day, I wondered why it was that I would retrieve my father's pajama pants and underwear out of his drawer before he would bathe. I never thought anything of it in my younger years, never thought it was strange or abnormal, because it's just something that I had always been asked to do. But looking back I wondered why I was touching my father's underwear? I wondered why he didn't get his own night clothes out. Nobody got mine or any other family member's sleeping attire out.

That being said, reliving the events of that night brought some things to the light for me. The realization of how cold my mother had been to me when I told her what my father had asked me. One would have thought that a mother would be extremely overprotective of their children and would do everything possible to protect them from predators. I guess I expected some empathy, compassion, and love from my mother that night.

Instead, she said nothing to me, but simply told my grandmother to take me to her house. And even when my grandmother brought me back home later in the night, there was still no reassurance that she would protect me from my father. In a sense, I kind of felt like a prisoner in my own home after that. But on the other hand, at least I was safely locked away from my father and oldest brother.

I hated when I would be made to come down from my room to even eat dinner. Every time I saw my father, it made my insides shake, and I remember being timid and scared when I had to be around him. In one brief moment, he had robbed me of my dad. It was crazy to think that I always felt safest in my father's presence, yet then he was the person that I feared the most. How could my mother allow him back in the home the very next day? Did she love him so much that she was willing to put me in harm's way? Did she feel so guilty that she wasn't performing for her husband anymore due to her health? And if that was the case, then was she willing to sacrifice me to my father for her own shortcomings? Why was it that every time I had come to talk to her about someone doing sexual things to me, why didn't she ever confront any of my predators, nor made any attempt to stop it? Maybe she didn't love me. I felt as though from a young age I felt violated, unloved, unwanted, and overall like she resented me in some way.

I just remembered spending the rest of our existence in that house locked away from everyone. How did I go downstairs and watch TV with my parents past that point, knowing that my father wanted to do disgusting things to me, and knowing that my mother was obviously okay with it? I never understood all the crazy disgusting behavior going on in my family, or how nobody ever intervened and put a stop to it. It was during my reflecting back, that I realized that maybe my mother didn't deserve to be held on the pedestal that Jayson and I had held her on since her death. In fact, I had come to the moment when I stopped mourning the loss of my mother and realized how hurt I felt by her constant inability to protect me and at that moment I felt much anger and rage towards her.

Now I understand how sick my mother was my entire life, because I provided most of her care while she was home. But I'm sorry, nothing excuses the horror that we kids grew up living every day of our childhood. In fact, it was her job above anyone else's to nurture and protect her children, because she is the one who chose to carry each one of us to term and then chose to keep each one of us.

I myself, being a mother, would fight to the death to protect my children. I would go hungry so my kids could eat. Overall, minus the constant yelling between their father and myself, my kids had an amazing life compared to the one we lived. I always put them first. They never had to be made fun of by their peers because they had stains on their clothes or holes in them. I kept my kids safe and always encouraged them in their education and extracurricular activities. I truly would kill someone if they hurt my children, and I would smile at the judge and tell him, "Yes, I did it, and I'd do it again." Now that's how strong a mother's love for her children should be. If my mother didn't love us kids like that, then why didn't she give us up? Oh that's right, then she and my father wouldn't have had anyone to support the two of them, or steal for them, or lie and cover up for them.

Over the years, I've walked around with this anger inside me, like a ticking time bomb waiting to explode.

Next I reflected on moving from this house where I was able to keep myself safe, locked away behind closed doors, and into the next place. I ran away almost immediately after moving to this house. I was terrified of running away, but what was the alternative? Stay there 100% unprotected from my oldest brother and father? No, I had made the decision on the day that I left, that I would have to test the waters of what my mother had burned into my mind all those years, "Shhh….. We can't talk about that or they'll take you away and we'll never see each other again." I decided that was a risk that I'd just have to take. Besides I was 13, and knew who my parents and siblings were, so how could it be that we'd never see each other again?

And how dare they make me endure and keep such an ugly secret all those years? I recalled the police finding me and telling me to go home, and me refusing and telling them the truth about why I didn't want to be there anymore. On that day, when I finally revealed the big secret, I saved myself from ever having to endure all the sick twisted abuse that I had endured all those years. I remember being in the locked psych ward for a couple of weeks until I got the news that I was gonna be transported to a foster home. I was terrified and angry, because I didn't want to go to a foster home. Why should I be punished when I hadn't done anything wrong?

Why should I have to be put in a foster home because of their actions? Scared, I took the short ride to meet my new foster mother and foster sister, little did I know my foster mother would be my saving grace.

Chapter 31
Barb My Savior

Walking into Barb's home that day, which was December 23rd 1987, I was scared, not knowing what to expect. Barb introduced herself to me as well as her daughter and then asked her daughter to show me where I would be sleeping. She told me to take some time and look around and then we could sit down and talk. She had a beautiful home and it smelled amazing from the candles that were burning. I slowly wandered through the apartment, familiarizing myself with where things were. When I finally went in and took a seat on the sofa, Barb asked me if I was ready to talk a little and get to know each other a little better. In conversation, she asked me if I smoked cigarettes, I answered honestly, expecting her to tell me that I wasn't allowed to smoke in her home. But instead, what she said next, kind of shocked me. She then asked what brand I smoked. I told her that I smoke Marlboro Reds, and she said to me, "Well let's go down to the store and get you some." At first, I thought that I didn't hear her correctly, until she said, "Get your shoes on and I'll meet you in the car."

As I came outside to join Barb in her car, she was just bee-bopping to some music that was blaring from the speakers as she sang at the top of her lungs, dancing and snapping her fingers in her little white Plymouth horizon with yellow pinstripes. My first thought was "This woman is crazy," but hey she was cool with me smoking, so at least I didn't have to hide it from her or worry about her smelling it on me. She bought me an entire carton of Marlboro reds. That definitely earned her some brownie points with me, even if she danced and sang to her interesting music all the way to the store and back.

Still a bit nervous about being there, Barb said to me, "C'mon sweetie, let's go see what clothes we can find you in my room, so you can take a shower and put on something comfortable to sleep in tonight." She told me to freshen up and that I could use whatever soaps and shampoos and conditioner I wished to use in the bathroom. And she also said if I didn't like any of the ones that they had there, then they could get me my own. And she also told me that a couple of days after Christmas, she would be receiving money for a clothing allowance for me, and then we could go shopping. It was actually like $700 or somewhere around that number.

However, we needed to get past the holiday first. As I sat there and thought about the holiday two days away, I felt anxious. My brain was picking apart a hundred questions about the holiday. I wondered if I would get to see my mom on Christmas. If not, what would I do? Sit and watch them open presents? I didn't know if I could do that. I hated the imposing "holiday." I had a lot that I wanted to know about rules and if I'd be able to see my family, or talk to them on the phone. What about Jayson, could I talk to him? I really wanted to ask Barb these questions, yet there I sat silent as a church mouse while my head was whirling with different scenarios. Since I spent a lot of my childhood alone in my room, I hadn't learned how to say what was on my mind, or how I was feeling, or how to approach people with conversation, or how to ask for help with anything. I wasn't able to be a child; instead, I was a very sad and lonely caregiver, thief, garbage digger, and an overall source of income for my father and mother. Oh yeah, and my being made let's not forget my being made to be my oldest brother's sex slave. Perhaps that seemed a little harsh, but wasn't that what I was? I felt sadness many times when my mother stayed in the hospital and her condition worsened. I couldn't tell you even a ballpark number of times that my mother was admitted to the ICU unit in the hospital or was classified as being on her deathbed and not expected to make it another day at best. I had a lot to think about, worry about, and be sad about as a child.

On Christmas morning, Barb woke the two of us. I was dreading going downstairs to watch the two of them open gifts. She had us sit on the couch and then she said, "Well, since Rose is the newest addition to our family, I think we have to let her go first," "Go first?" I ask myself. "Go first at what?" I was sitting there, looking a bit baffled as Barb handed me a present. I wasn't quite sure how to respond, so I just sat there awkwardly holding the present, as I was looking at the floor, and I almost in a whisper responded with a "thank you".

"Well what are you waiting for?" she asked. "Go ahead and open it," she said. I couldn't tell you today what that first gift was, but I would say by the end of the gift unwrapping, I literally opened as many gifts as her daughter. I wondered where she had gotten the gifts from, or when she had even had time to buy me gifts. I did like the new things I had gotten that day, but I felt extremely awkward receiving the presents. There had only been one previous Christmas where there were gifts to exchange and be unwrapped. I did get to visit with my mother for a couple of hours in the afternoon, before returning back to my new temporary home.

It was a couple of days later when as promised, that Barb had received a clothing allowance for me, and we went clothing and shoe shopping. We went to approximately 4 different stores, and at each one, I would choose some clothes that I liked and would try them on in the dressing room, and then come out so Barb could see how they looked and make sure that they fit me okay. I hadn't ever gone clothing shopping, much less tried clothes on in a changing room. Barb helped me pick clothes that would fit me in a way that was best for my size and that would cover my stomach and the other larger parts of my body that I always felt insecure about, because, since the age of 10, when I developed and started putting on weight, I was called fat by my peers. So, I did have a lot of insecurities. I remember wearing jeans that were way too small on me hoping that they would hide some of my fat, but it didn't do me any justice due to the jeans cutting me in half practically and the rest of my stomach just bulged over the top of the jeans. And then I would wear clothes that were extremely big and would just hang off of me. Barb helped me find clothes that actually fit me, that weren't too big or too small. I really had fun shopping with Barb that day. But we were both exhausted by the time we got home.

I was so excited to start school after winter break. At least by then, I would have nice, new, non-stained clothes and shoes that didn't have holes in them. And I got to start my new school with a new book bag and school supplies. I felt so good on my first day at my new school, that is until someone yells, "Who's the new girl?" And then the comment that followed that was the exact reason that I was so insecure. As I walked down the hall another kid yelled, "BOOM.....BOOM....BOOM.....Save the Whales." Now if that doesn't shoot down one's confidence and take away the glow I felt when I left the house that morning. When I went to gym class a couple days later, we had to change our clothes in the locker room into our gym clothes. And then at the end of gym class, there were showers so we could get the sweat off us before putting our street clothes back on. It only took 1 gym class for me to refuse to dress out for gym class ever again.

Because as I tried to shower like all the other girls, I was laughed at and pointed at and made to feel like a spectacle. I tried to just focus on my classes while at school, because when not in the classroom the taunting never stopped. I recall on several occasions that there would be rumors going around that I was pregnant.

As my birthday rolled around on the 20th of January 1988, I had my first-ever birthday party. All of Barb's family came to the party and brought me gifts and cards with money in them. But what was more important to me was the way that Barb's entire family accepted me as a member of their family.

That felt really good because none of them had to open up their hearts or families to me. Barb asked me how I would like my hair for my party and I told her I really wanted a perm, but that unfortunately, they didn't ever seem to stay in my hair for more than a couple weeks. Barb however had me wash my hair with Dawn dish soap. She said that this would strip the medicine and other toxins out of my hair allowing the perm to take better. My perm did indeed stay nearly 6 months this time. I was elated.

As winter quickly turned into spring, we moved from the apartment to a house in Lincoln Way Village, which is a neighborhood near the local community college. We had a little more room and a yard here. Before long Barb had her pop-up camper at Jolly Rogers campground near Iowa City, IA. We spent a lot of time there between the spring, summer, and fall. Barb was all about being around her brothers and sister and all the nieces and nephews. I really enjoyed camping, well besides setting up and tearing down the pop-up camper.

I recalled once when we were at Jolly Rogers Campgrounds, Jayson came to visit me. As he entered, you could very clearly and loudly hear my name being bellowed. He had a PA system hooked up to his car, so he kept speaking through it, "Rose, where are you?" "You can't hide from me." "Sissy, hello?" As he pulled up to the same camping spot where Barb's camper always sat, he said, "Hi Sissy." "Will you turn that stupid thing off?" I asked him. Then he hit the horn, which could play about 25 different tunes when honked. He had always been obnoxious, and it made me want to crawl into a hole and hide. He then tried to teach me how to drive a stick shift. Let's just say I didn't get the car to move very far, but instead threw up some grass and dirt with the spinning tires. I was just glad my brother had come to see me.

Barb never stopped me from having my brother as an active support system in my life, and Jayson had a lot of love and respect for Barb as well. I recalled one day, due to Barb's initials, which just so happened to be BMW, Jayson said to me, "Do you know what, Sissy?" "What, Jayson?" I responded. He said, "I've always wanted to drive a BMW." "You're retarded," I responded. And from that day forward, he always tried to get me to tell Barb that he wanted to drive a BMW. There wasn't any way I was going to say that to Barb. However, years later, when he called my phone while I was visiting Barb, I told him where I was, and he again said to me,

"Tell Barb I want to drive a BMW." I laughed this time and handed my phone to Barb, saying, "Here, Jayson wants to tell you something." She said, "Hello," and the next thing I heard her say was, "You think you're pretty funny, huh?" "I hope you know you're still not too big to bend over my knee and spank your ass." Granted, I may have begged to differ with Barb at this point; she hadn't seen my brother in years, and he definitely wasn't the scrawny little kid she had last seen. He was about a solid 265 pounds of grown man at this point. It was super funny; Jayson finally got a chance to say to her what he had begged me to tell her for years.

I stayed in contact with Barb all the way up to when she passed due to complications from diabetes. She held true to the promise she had made to me all those years ago as we stood crying, holding each other the day the state of Iowa placed me back in my father's care. She promised me that her home and phone would always be open to me and that she would always be there if I needed her.

Still to this day, I find myself wanting to pick up the phone to call her. And to my beloved foster mom, this is what I want to say: "Barb, thank you so much for opening your home and heart not only to me but to many others. I honestly don't know where I would be today without the love and guidance you showed me. There isn't a day that goes by that I don't miss you, though I know you will forever be in my memories and in my heart. To this day, you are my hero. I love you and miss you so much, but I know you will be there waiting with your loving embrace one day when we reunite. Until we meet again."

Chapter 32

As I reflected back at my last memories of my youth years, it brought me back to nothing more than my oldest brother. The things that I was forced to let him do to me for all those years, have never faded from my memory. The day I left his house all those years ago, after waking yet again to him knelt beside where I slept, I was scared. I wasn't scared about where I would go next in my journeys in life, but afraid of the vicious thoughts that ran through my mind following that incident.

Suicidal thoughts were something that always haunted me. However, I had homicidal thoughts that haunted my mind every time I thought about what my oldest brother and five of my cousins did to me, as well as the question my father asked me when I was just 12 years old.

I made it clear to my oldest brother and my father after that, that I would kill either one of them if they ever in the future came at me again in a sexual manner. And I mean every word of that still to this day. I hate hearing stories of rape, sexual assaults, and child molesters on the news. It angers me to my deepest core. And I understand that what I'm going to say next is going to sound extremely dark and twisted, but I can honestly say that over the years, I have fantasized about torturing sexual predators. And it scares me that those thoughts excite me in some kind of way, but it's the truth.

So, I had to learn to balance all these years, not only the suicidal thoughts but also the homicidal thoughts. I told many therapists and psychiatrists over the years that if I told someone two times not to touch me, or if I said "no" twice, that was once too many, and I wasn't responsible for my actions at that point. I was extremely overprotective of my daughter, who am I kidding, I still am. Some people thought I was too extreme with how protective I had been when it came to her, because I sheltered her so much. However, for me, I can honestly say that nobody took my daughter's innocence as mine was taken from me, and to me, that was my biggest accomplishment of raising both of my children.

I am begging to people with young children, "Please talk to your children about predators, and what a good touch versus a bad touch is. Set up a game plan with your children on what your expectations are for them if they ever encounter one of these predators in the course of their life. Reassure them that you will make sure that they are safe from that person ever hurting them again."

And another thing, parents, please ensure that that predator is held accountable if your child comes to you and tells you that someone is hurting them. It's funny how nobody ever wants to talk about sexual predators, so incidents become big "family secrets." Fuck that, expose those mother fuckers, because you may be many other children's saving grace by exposing them. Why do predators end up having so many victims? Because nobody wants to expose them, or because they don't want the humility of others knowing what their family may be dealing with as a result of a predator. As for me, I don't know if one of my children or grandchildren were to endure sexual abuse that I could let it go until that individual was six feet under and would never hurt anyone again. And please, the last thing I would ask of parents is to please stop letting your kids grow up too fast.

Instead, always encourage them to enjoy their youth, because in life we really only get a short window of time to be young and carefree, something I, unfortunately, didn't get to experience in my life.

For years I wondered what had happened to my oldest brother, or where he had learned to do all those things that he did to me during his middle of the night visits. However, just a couple of years ago, when Jayson overdosed hopefully for the last time, I believe I got the answer to those looming questions.

Jayson was found that day by my nephew. He was found sitting naked on his living room floor rocking and kept saying things that didn't make much sense to anyone. He had stopped taking all of his psych meds for schizophrenia and such for ten days, and had spent them ten days smoking amphetamines. He had at some point aspirated on his vomit for what was now his second time through four overdoses.

When he arrived by ambulance at St. Lukes Hospital I was alerted that he was there. As I entered the emergency room that day, I witnessed my brother flailing about unable to stop the involuntary jerking that his body kept doing. His lips and tongue were both swollen and he was fairly red around his mouth and eyes. Immediately as I entered the room, I could hear my brother saying my father's name over and over again. I actually recorded about two twenty-second videos of Jayson that day, because I wanted him to see the things that I have to see during his overdoses. You can hear him saying my father's name repeatedly in the videos.

As he continued to say my father's name, I thought to myself, "What about him?" Did my father go to my brother's apartment that day and do something bad to him? However, the more I thought about that scenario, I realized that was fairly unlikely, as it seemed my father hadn't ever been to any of my brother's places where he lived. Nor had he ever known where Jayson lived or had his phone number, for that matter.

As time progressed that day in the ER, Jayson went from just repeatedly saying my father's name to now he was squeezing and shaking my arm saying "Sissy, ******", which was my father's name. As I looked into my brother's face that day, I saw a very young Jayson. The questions and thoughts that swarmed my head at that time, would have to wait until a later day, as the nurses struggled to even keep leads on Jayson, as he couldn't stop his body from jerking and was quite combative. They told me that they would try to give Jayson some medicine to sedate him, when another hospital staff member entered the room and told me that there was an individual in the waiting room claiming to be Jayson's father. I walked out in the hall with her and I explained to her that he was not Jayson's father but mine instead. Yes, Jayson has always had his last name, but that's because when he and our mother got together, she was two months pregnant with Jayson and she married my father a month later, hence why Jayson had his last name. I also stressed to her not to allow him to come back to the room, with as combative as Jayson already was, and the fact that he was so adamant about trying to tell me something about my father, I couldn't imagine how Jayson would have reacted had he walked into the room that day.

They ended up telling my father that they were struggling with Jayson and they didn't think it was a good idea to allow anyone else back in the room at that point. He got tired of sitting in the waiting room and eventually went home.

The doctors and nurses tried about four different cocktails that day in the effort to sedate my brother. All of which were unsuccessful. Which meant that they were unable to run any tests to find out what was going on with him. They finally asked my permission to put my brother in a medically induced coma so that they could run the necessary tests to find out what had caused him to act the way he was so that they could begin the appropriate treatments that he needed. As much as I hated the sight of my brother being on life support I reluctantly agreed.

Eventually, he was moved to the intensive care unit. I was vigilantly at his bedside, again wondering if my brother would pull through again this time and wondering how much more damage he had done to his brain and body.

The following day, one of my nieces who came to see him, apparently ran a video of Jayson on the ventilator, and let's just say that that video spread quickly via the internet to all of my other nieces and nephews as well as to my father's household.

So unaware of said video, as I sat there with Jayson my phone rang. I didn't even bother to look at the phone number that was calling, instead I just answered it. I hear the individual on the other end ask "How is he?" Honestly, the voice in my ear sounded like our oldest cousin from our mother's side of the family. I gave a brief update and all of a sudden the individual on the other end of the line started sobbing saying, "He's nothing like I remember him." I then realized who it was that I was talking to and quickly hung up the phone. It had been our oldest brother that had called me that day.

Let me just say for the record that Jayson hates our oldest brother with every inch of his being. Not only because of having to deal with how fucked up I was behind all the sexual abuse that I endured with him through our childhood, but also finding my niece performing oral sex to her brother not to mention, having heard her say that she liked to have sex with her father and his girlfriend at the time when he disappeared in the middle of the night not to be seen or heard from for many years to come.

Jayson told his therapist and psychiatrist many times that if he ever saw our oldest brother again, he would kill him. They alerted Florida authorities to inform them if he returned to Iowa there was a fairly remarkable threat on his life.

So, let's just say with the realization of who I had just spoken with on the phone, I called all of my nieces and nephews to find out if any of them had contacted our oldest brother. When I placed a call to my father, I then knew who it was that had called our oldest brother that day. I asked him why he had called and told him about Jayson, and he responded, "because that's his brother." I replied, "He is not our brother anymore." "Well, I disagree," he said back to me. I said, "Do you realize that Jayson fucking hates him and if he ever sees him, he WILL KILL HIM?" I then asked him, "So, if you keep getting updates about Jayson, are you going to continue updating him?" "Yes, I am," he said back to me. I then said, "Well check this out, my brother can't speak for himself at the moment, so I will see to it that his wishes are respected. Furthermore, you will not be getting any more updates on Jayson." "Well, I'm going to contact a lawyer on Monday." "What for?" I asked him. He said, "because you won't let me see my son." "That's not your son," I replied back. “Well, I raised him,” he said. “Did you really? Did you really raise us? Is that what it’s called?” I asked him and I hung up the phone. From that point forward, only two nephews and one niece could call the hospital or visit besides myself.

Chapter 33

Thankfully again, Jayson did pull through. Not sure how he kept defeating the odds over and over again, but just like every other overdose, I knew it was gonna be a long journey back to health, but elated to say the least.

On the Mother's Day, the following year after Jayson started his road to recovery, I had an amazing day with both of my kids, starting with brunch and game time at the local Pizza Ranch, followed by picking up my son at the flower shop he worked at. I remember he was super excited to show me pictures of him walking around with a macaw on his shoulder that a customer had come into the store with. We then went to my favorite Mexican restaurant, where the three of us all had a frozen margarita, and it was the first drink that we got to share together since both the kids were of legal age. We sat there for a couple of hours and ate our meals and talked and of course, the presents that the kids had given me.

When we were finished at the restaurant, my daughter got in her car, and my son decided that he'd like to ride with me. As we were riding around, my son asked me if I would stop at my stepsister's house, cause he wanted to see her. This also just so happened to be where my father was living. My one stepsister came outside and brought me a wine cooler. As we sat there chatting while drinking the wine coolers, she said to me, "Dad said next time you come around, he'd like to talk to you." As I sat there, at the moment when she spoke those words, I found myself at a pivotal point in this book, having just revisited my youth by introducing you to the younger version of myself.

I thought about the wonderful day I had just had with my kids, and I thought about what I wanted to say to him from the last time I had spoken to him when I shut down updates to him about Jayson's care and progress. I was gonna stand up for my brother when I spoke to my father. My step-sister went inside to see if he was still awake.

As I saw him come out on the porch, I got out of my truck and walked across the street. As I approached him, I said to him, "You know, this is what I have to say about Jayson's last overdose, and me not letting you have updates on him." I then said to him, "You made that personal between you and I, when in reality, it didn't have anything to do with us. It was about being my brother's voice when he could not, and respecting his wishes. The person that you called that day to tell him about Jayson, is not our brother anymore. Period." And I told him if he couldn't respect our wishes then he doesn't have to be part of our lives." I then said to him, "Do you know my brother can't stand you?" "Oh yeah?", he responded back. "Why is that?" "Oh, I don't know, maybe because you've never been there for him for starters," I said to him. "Oh, I haven't, have I?" he replied. "No, you never have been there for him. Let's talk about this. Do you understand that you and he have basically lived in the same city since our mother died in 1988? Have you ever gone to visit him? Ever known where he lived or what his address was? Ever have his phone number? Nope, but you surely have your pedophile son's number on speed dial. I guess birds of a feather really do stick together," I said to him. Then I said to him, "As a matter of fact, my brother went to prison, what do you think he went there for? Oh that's right, for stealing, what you and our mother not only taught us to do, but made us do for you. Did you ever go visit him or maybe put some money on his books?" "You know, since you're the ones that programmed us to steal. Shit, I think that's the least you could do considering the circumstances. So, again, no, you never have been there for my brother," I said to him.

I guess I was feeling liberated after standing up to my father about my brother, because I then said to him, "Since I have you here, there are a few other things I'd like to discuss with you." I then said to him, "Do you know that I have social anxiety as a result of my peers tormenting me because I was sent to school wearing rags and outdated clothing?" He replied back to me, "So I suppose that's my fault huh?" I ignored his question and continued on. "And then you guys started making us climb into garbage cans and dumpsters in front of our peers to get cans and bottles for you and our mother." "So now we were called garbage diggers." "So I suppose that's my fault too?" he asked me. This time his question pissed me off and I replied, "Yes mother fucker, it is."

I figured since I already started confronting him about things from my youth that have never left me, I might as well keep going. I might not have another opportunity to confront him about these things. "The next thing I'd like to discuss with you is my seventh birthday. Now I knew not to expect parties, gifts, cake, and ice cream, or anything like that, because there was never money for that, but did you know I went to school on my seventh birthday, and not a single person from my family told me happy birthday that morning?" I asked him. "So needless to say, I went through my school day feeling sad. However, when I walked into the house after school that day, there you sat, in all your glory, paddle in hand. I still remember the words you said to me that day." "Bet you thought I forgot what today was huh? Time for your birthday spanking." "You were so glad to see me that day," I said. "As you swung that 1" by 4" board that you had made into a paddle the first time that day, I was in tears. You laughed and carried on and had such a good time, and with each swing, you swung harder." I said to him, "After that, I cried myself to sleep, and walked around black and blue for the next couple weeks."

"Another thing I'd like to talk about is the MDA." "When I lived at J Street apartments, I decided to drive down the hill to the gas station to get some cigarettes and something to drink. As I came down the hill, I could see that the firefighters were at the corner collecting donations in their boots. I said to the one firefighter that I would stop on my way back out. As promised, I dropped like seven dollars and some change in his boot, and he handed me a sticker. I happened to look at the sticker as I drove back up the hill. The sticker read "I donated to the MDA." Let's just say I was sobbing by the time I drove the one block back home that day, because I know how much you and our mother made us steal from that organization as children." "Well you guys got something out of it didn't you?" he responded. "Does that freaking make it right? We were children," I screamed at him. By this point his wife came out for what was the second time that day and she said, "Okay ******, it's time to come in and go to bed now, and Rose, you can leave." I said, "What I am here talking to him about, doesn't have anything to do with you, because you weren't present." "Well you're not the one that has to hold him at night while he cries," she said to me. "I wish the fuck I would," I responded back. "He's supposed to be a grown ass man. Who has been wiping my tears since the age of three? Get the fuck outta here," I said as I turned around and walked away. Now I didn't exactly expect intelligent answers that day as I confronted my father about things from my childhood, so I wasn't disappointed. But it felt so good to finally get that stuff off my chest. I'd carried that extra baggage around for years, and it finally felt that the weight of the world that I'd carried on my shoulders for all those years, was finally starting to lighten up.

Chapter 34

Since Jayson's last overdose had been at least six months ago, I chose to talk to him about the day he was taken to the emergency room. So I said to him, "I have a question. Did my dad ever do anything to you sexually when you were younger?" "No," he responded, "If he did Sissy, I would tell you." I said, "Well the reason I'm asking is because the day you were brought to St Lukes, you kept saying my father's name. As a matter of fact, I ran two short videos in the ER that day, because I really want you to see and understand what I go through every time you do this. In the videos you can hear you plain as the day saying his name. You then went from just saying his name that day, to literally grabbing my arm squeezing and shaking it saying, "Sissy ******." So, what if you don't remember in your conscious mind?" I asked him. "What if you've locked it away to protect yourself because it was too traumatic? When I looked into your face that day as you squeezed and shook my arm, Jayson, I saw an extremely young you," I said. "You were extremely adamant about telling me something about my father that day. I've spent a lot of time since then thinking about things, Jayson. However, I wanted to give you some time to heal before bringing this conversation to you. There's not a doubt in my mind that he did indeed do something to both of you boys. Well our oldest brother, because of all the things he did to me when we were all super young. Someone had to teach him those things. And I never would have thought anything happened to you until that day in the ER," I said. "It would explain a lot, Jayson. The schizophrenia, how you and he hated each other our whole lives, and your constant need to numb yourself." "It does make sense Sissy, but I don't remember anything," he said to me.

As a little more time went by, Jayson ended up living with me for a while. One day he said to me, "You know Sissy, I think you may be right about your dad. I've been trying to think as hard as I can to see if I can remember anything." "I don't think that's a good idea Jayson, your mind locked that away for a reason to protect you. I don't think it will end well if the images of whatever happened comes back to you. I honestly don't think you could handle that, and sadly I think that would be the end of you Jayson. Please don't keep trying to bring it back." Another day a couple months later after he got his own apartment again, he called me and said, "Check this out Sissy, I've been sitting here thinking about the day I overdosed, and I remember I was thinking about your dad. I don't exactly recall what my thoughts were about him, but I do remember thinking about him before I don't remember what happened the rest of that day, and until I woke up in the ICU when you were there."

Undoubtedly, there's not a question in my mind after all of it that my father did something awful to both the boys. I've added everything up over and over, yet every time it leads right back to him. His story he used to tell about when the boys were in diapers, that they had taken their diapers off and sat with a hammer and the one would grab the other's privates and hit it with a hammer and then they would switch off, "And they laughed and laughed," he said each time he told the story.

Truthfully, what was really going on. It was after the conversation with my brother and another family member who told me that my father had touched them also that I decided I just can't see or talk to my father anymore. All those years since my mother's death, I chased a relationship with my father. And for what? To be honest, he should have been honored that I ever had anything to do with him after he asked to stick his dick in me when I was 12 years old.

I'm not ashamed of what I went through in the past. Disgusted is a more accurate word.

Disgusted that I had parents that were so fucked up to have brought any of us into the world. We basically were born for a welfare check and to steal to support the house. My entire childhood for the eight years that we lived in the Ft Madison area, I only recall my father having two jobs, each only lasting a couple of months. Come to think of it, I even recall having to climb into the dumpster at the local Aldi grocery store to get expired packaged food items that they had thrown away.

Life has never been easy trying to overcome the damage done from the neglect and abuse that we lived through in our childhood. It's taken a long time to do so many things. Such as how to communicate. I always held all my thoughts and feelings in, because I wasn't allowed to have a voice or opinion when I was younger. I'd hold everything in until I would blow up while trying to communicate my feelings to someone. I didn't know healthy ways to communicate. In crowds of people, I've always been quiet and timid. Not having the courage to speak up.

Relationships have been a struggle for me as well. I've always been insecure and been a people pleaser in a sense. I've also always been the person that takes care of everyone and everything. I used to be easily guilt tripped and manipulated by men. In fact, I have had a couple physically abusive relationships. In both cases neither of them worked, but yet tried to control and manipulate me by being aggressive towards me. However, at the end of my last domestic abuse relationship, he went to prison after the county attorney hit him with three felony domestics at the same time following three assaults within a two-week period.

I recall asking a therapist once why I keep choosing the same kind of men, and this is what she said to me, "Well, you see Rose, as young girls, it is our father's responsibility to lay the foundation for us on how we should be treated by men in the future." Mine sure did that for me, didn't he? This has taken many years and a lot of failed relationships to improve.

I'd say the main factor is working on my self-esteem and figuring out my self-worth. I've always felt fat, ugly, not worthy of anything, and I felt a lot like I've in a sense tried to buy love, or tried really hard to please the man that I was with by allowing them to guilt trip me into buying them things or doing what they wanted me to do, so that they wouldn't leave. One day, while Jayson and I were talking he said to me, "Our whole lives, you've gone in search of love and happiness, why is that?" As I thought about what he had just said, I responded, "You know Jayson, what does the word love even mean? Mom told us a lot as children that she loved us, what we lived through, that's not love. So, I guess I've just always wanted one person to love me unconditionally, like I envision what love is." I can honestly say today that the overly emotional feeling I felt when they laid each of my children in my arms and I looked down into their tiny faces the day they were born, that is what love is. Many people use that word so fluently and just use it as a term of endearment, but for me it's so much more than a word. If I love someone, that means they have the ability to affect my emotions.

Another thing Jayson said to me several times over the years is, "Sissy, if there is one thing I could give you in life, it would be self-esteem, because you're a beautiful person inside and out." With Whitney Houston's song, Greatest Love of All, being my favorite song since the age of ten and the song that gave me the courage to push through all the horrible abuse, it isn't until recently that I've begun listening to the chorus…... "Learning to love yourself, that is the greatest love of all." Self-love is something that I've worked extremely hard on over the course of writing this book. I must say with self-love; you stop letting people walk all over you. You stop allowing men to disrespect you.

Recently, as I joined my brother one night for karaoke, he sang this song with me, and the chorus finally spoke to me as it never had before. It meant the world to me to have my brother sing it with me, knowing how significant that song has always been a staple in my life.

Chapter 35

In my life I have walked through the shadows of the valley of death. I have lived some of the most unimaginable and horrific things, but I'm not a victim, at least not anymore. I'm a warrior. The battles I have had to live through over the years have made me stronger, and more driven to help others who are struggling with finding enough fight within themselves to keep pushing through whatever life's demons have in store for them. I'm grateful that despite everything, I still have a good heart and that it hasn't just left me withdrawn and bitter. I still have the ability to love. Life truly has given me every reason to quit. But if I quit, then all these people that have administered so much hurt to me in my life, they will win. They've taken enough from me, they don't get my life too.

I've been told a lot in my life that I need to "get over it" or "leave the past in the past," or "that I have to forgive these people." Who is anyone to tell me how to heal the scars that I carry in my soul?

In fact, I was recently told by someone I thought would always be by my side that I only speak of my past for attention. No, definitely not for attention. First, because I think every predator should be put on blast in this world, because the sooner they are revealed and held accountable, the fewer victims they will have. Second, to heal my inner child by talking about it. And third, hopefully, I can help another lost and injured soul to keep fighting. In life, we all have to find our own reason to get up every day. For me, that reason is my children as well as my brother, Jayson. I'm not sure where I'd be without the three of them. We may not always see eye to eye on things, and we may get on each other's nerves, but they truly are my reason to not give up. No matter how good today is, always hope and strive for a better day tomorrow.

To my children.......

Thank you for showing me what love feels like. From the moment I saw you, I knew I loved you. I know that over the years, dealing with me on my mental health days hasn't always been the easiest thing, but you never gave up on me. It's truly my honor to call myself your mother. I'm so proud of the loving, wonderful adults you have each become. I just hope that you both believe in yourselves as much as I believe in you. The sky's the limit and the world is yours to conquer, and I'll be beside you every step of the way, encouraging you and cheering you on. I love you both beyond words.

To my Aunt LuAnn,

Thank you so much for always showing up and being there for Jayson and me when we felt our worlds caving in around us or when we thought we had nobody. One of your hugs has a way of squeezing all the broken pieces together. You've listened when I needed to vent or cry. Or even when I was bored and just wanted someone to BS with over the phone. And you've even gotten on my case when I needed someone to shake me out of a depressed self-pity episode. You didn't have to have anything to do with either of us since our mother's death, but you have. We both know that your door has always been open to us anytime, or that you're only a phone call away. I love you, Aunt LuAnn, even if not by blood, you'll always be my aunt. I love you, and thank you so much for all you've done for my brother and me in our lives.

To Barb......

Thank you for everything you represented and stood for. I hope I can impact people's lives in the way that you left your fingerprint on so many people's souls. If I could touch even one person's life the way you touched mine, that would be great. But I hope to touch many others' lives and leave behind a legacy as you did. I hope I make you proud. Until we meet again, please watch over me and continue to guide me with your loving spirit. I can't ever thank you enough for allowing me into your life. I love you so much, and miss you even more.

Last but not least, to my brother… Wow, where do I even start? As I am now staring down the barrel of my 50th birthday, I'm so glad that you're still by my side. I never thought you'd be around to not only see your 50th but now to see me through the half-century mark. We've had so many good times as well as bad times, but my love for you has never faltered. Some days we can't stand one another, or do things that piss the other one off, or say something that hurts the other one's feelings, but we're all each other has had in our lives consistently since my birth.

Without your love, I don't know where I'd be. You have loved me when I wasn't very lovable. I've always known that you are my biggest supporter. Thank you for allowing me to talk to you about all the sexual abuse that you didn't learn much about until a certain someone resurfaced in Cedar Rapids, bringing all those horrible demons from the past to light. You've spent countless hours listening to me as I have screamed and cried through reliving my childhood in my quest to heal from the scars that sat deep in my soul. And thank you for giving up the drugs so that I can still have you by my side until our dying days. From the worst imaginable to the most memorable, I wouldn't have wanted to take this journey with anyone else. And always know that even when I shut down from time to time and block everyone out while I work through something that's bothering me in my personal life, I'll never leave you or shut you out of my life forever. Thank you for everything, Jayson. I love you more than I could ever put into words.

You are my ride or die from beginning to end. Let's just not make the end for many more years to come. Let's make the second half-century the best it can be. I love you always and forever, to infinity and beyond.

P.S. I just want to give everyone a quick update. Upon the completion of my book two months ago, there are a couple revelations that have came to light. After my son had attended a family funeral that I was unable to attend due to work, he started saying things to me like, "Grandpa didn't come to the funeral because he can't walk or get around very well right now." "Grandma says the doctors have given Grandpa less than three years to live." "Grandma says she'd like to see you and talk to you again sometime before they pass away." The more I kept replaying the things my son had said to me through my mind, I thought, my issue isn't with my step mom, it's with my dad. Well since my son seemed to be going over to a family member's house quite a bit, which just so happened to be where his grandparents were currently staying also, I text my son one night after work and asked what he was doing. He responded back, "playing Uno." I automatically knew where he was, so I said, "I was thinking about walking over, but that's quite the walk, so I don't know if I can walk all the way there and then back home." He said, "Just come over here Mom. I'll let you ride my bike back home."

So, I headed out the door and began my walk. The reason I decided to go there that night was because I decided that there were some more things I'd like to say to my father while he was still alive instead of waiting until his funeral. I sat and just kinda visited with my step siblings and my step mom for maybe 15 minutes. My father was sitting at the table with the rest of them and I was sitting back to the left side of where he sat. I couldn't see his face, but I began talking to my stepmom and I said to her, "I know you've been wondering why I haven't been around. Well it's kind of like this, if I'm going to be around my father, then he's going to have to start answering some questions. And to be honest, I'm not sure I want the details on some things." I then told her about Jayson's last overdose and how Jayson arrived at the hospital saying my father's name. Then how he went from just saying his name to squeezing and shaking my arm saying, "Sissy ******." and how when I looked into his face, it was like it morphed back to a very young Jayson. I said, "My brother was very adamant about trying to tell me something about my father that day.

Though he never got out what he wanted to tell me that day, I heard him loud and clear." I then said, "There's not a doubt in my mind that he didn't fuck with both of my brother's sexually when they were young." This man sat there silently. He didn't deny it. He didn't defend himself. He just sat there silent. I then said that I know about what he did to another family member, which made him squirm in his seat a little. I know he was confused about how I had knowledge of that situation.

So I said to my stepmother, "You see though, I don't want the details of what he did to my brothers when they were young, but do you know what I'd really like the answers to? I want to know why our oldest brother was not once disciplined for seven years of molesting me? He wasn't reprimanded or even talked to ever about the sexual shit. And I'd really like to know why there weren't any provisions put in place for my safety?" Still my father sat silent. I'm sorry, but to me, his silence is an admission of guilt. It makes me sick to my stomach, but just like the last time I confronted him it took so much weight off of my shoulders. Now I can truly say that I have spoken my last words to him.

Next, just a couple of weeks ago during a conversation with my son, we decided to see if we could find out what my cousin was back in prison for, since being taken back to Oklahoma by the marshals in 2008. My son said he couldn't find anything, so I told him to look it up in a different way, and he came across a news article about him. It appeared that after doing 20 years for rape and sodomy of a young boy, and prior to him coming back to Iowa, he had raped a little girl in Oklahoma.

Charged with 1st degree rape with instrumentation, and sentenced to two life sentences plus 200 years. Tears stung my eyes as my son read that article. Both for this young victim and how much therapy and such this poor baby would need in the future, and elated that he will never be allowed to do it again, since he will spend the rest of his days incarcerated.

Last but not least, about four days ago, my son called me and said, "Mom, it's about to be all over." "What are you talking about?' I asked him. He informed me that my father was on the phone with our oldest brother and that he told my father that he only has maybe two more months to live as he has stage four lung cancer. I told my son to call me back because I needed a couple minutes to process what he had just told me.

Jayson asked me to come over that night and sit with him while he placed a call to our oldest brother. He said "Sissy, I just want to see if on his deathbed if he's ready to come clean about the things he's done. I want to know if he has regrets and feels remorse for hurting you and others." He tried to call the number that my son had retrieved. There was no answer. Next Jayson's phone rang, and it was our oldest brother's wife on the other end. She said that he had taken his medication and was asleep, and that we could call back the next day. So, I went back to Jayson's in the morning. He made me place the call and speak to our oldest brother, "I'm sitting with Jayson, do you want to talk to him?" "Sure," he replied.

After they got past the initial "How are you's," Jayson said, "You left and went to Florida 27 years ago, while I was here dealing with the dysfunctionality in Rose and others as a result of what you did to them." Our oldest brother responded back, "If that's what you're going to talk about, then I'm going to hang up." Jayson said, "Okay do it then." And the call disconnected. Jayson then said, "I got the closure I needed. I guess he'll take it to his grave and die alone."

It's crazy how life plays out sometimes. I don't really wish death on people for the most part, but as of right now, today, I can say God is good. Let me explain, I didn't wish death upon at least two of them, yet they've both been dealt their final mortality. As for the other one, he's been dealt his fate.

In the end, none of the three main predators in my life would hurt anyone ever again. So for that reason I say, "God is good!"

The End...

Made in United States
Troutdale, OR
11/30/2024